The Elfreth
Book of Letters

EDITED, WITH AN INTRODUCTION, BY

Susan Winslow Hodge

FOREWORD BY ANTHONY N. B. GARVAN

The
Elfreth
Book
of
Letters

The Elfreth Book of Letters

EDITED, WITH AN INTRODUCTION, BY

Susan Winslow Hodge

FOREWORD BY ANTHONY N. B. GARVAN

UNIVERSITY OF PENNSYLVANIA PRESS

PHILADELPHIA

upp

Designed by Adrianne Onderdonk Dudden
Copyright © 1985 by The Elfreth's Alley Association, Inc.

Library of Congress Cataloging in Publication Data
Main entry under title:

The Elfreth book of letters.

Includes bibliographical references.
1. Children—Pennsylvania—Philadelphia—Social
conditions—Sources.   2. Friends, Society of—
Pennsylvania—Philadelphia—History—Sources.
3. Education of children—Pennsylvania—Philadelphia—
History—Sources.   4. Children's writings, American—
Pennsylvania—Philadelphia.   5. Elfreth family.
I. Hodge, Susan Winslow.
HQ792.U5E43   1985   305.2'3'0974811   84-1134
ISBN 0-8122-7982-4
ISBN 0-8122-1208-8 (pbk.)

Printed in the United States of America

*This book is dedicated
to the Robert T. Elfreth family,
for generously sharing
a bit of their family's history.*

Contents

Acknowledgments 9
Foreword by Anthony N. B. Garvan 11
Introduction 13

THE ELFRETH BOOK OF LETTERS 21

Afterword 176

Acknowledgments

Preparing *The Elfreth Book of Letters* for publication has involved the help of many people. Under the direction of presidents Elizabeth Gray Kogen and Celian B. Putnam, the 1984–85 Board of Directors of The Elfreth's Alley Association, Inc., strongly supported this project from its inception and made every resource of the Association available to ensure publication. Financial support was generously provided by The Quaker Chemical Foundation, whose contributions over the years have made a wide variety of Association projects possible. I am grateful to Ingalill Hjelm, Managing Editor of the University of Pennsylvania Press, for her valuable professional advice and guidance. I am particularly indebted to three people who were instrumental in seeing this project through to completion: my thanks to Peter J. Parker and Tony Garvan for conversation about the diary and its contents, and my thanks also to Trina Vaux, who was never too busy to share her understanding of the publication process with me.

I wish to thank Frank Margeson of the American Philosophical Society for photographing the *Book of Letters* in preparation for the printing process.

For advice, encouragement, and suggestions I would also like to thank my husband, Steve, who has listened to many a story of people, things, and places long since disappeared, and who alone understands the depth of my interest in the past.

Foreword

The study of Philadelphia's past, and indeed most historical writing in the United States during the past decade, has been marked as much by the discovery of new classes of evidence as by new formulations based upon traditional sources. The Elfreth's Alley Association and its Director, Susan Winslow Hodge, have once again exercised leadership by publishing, with the support of The Quaker Chemical Foundation, a day book or diary of children born between 1824 and 1830. In 1934 the Association initiated preservation of Elfreth's Alley, one of the first historical districts. Lined by preserved eighteenth-century dwellings, the alley also boasts a well-crafted historical museum. It remains today one of the very few historically preserved areas devoted to urban craftsmen.

The Elfreth children were distant descendants of Jeremiah Elfreth, who owned several houses on the alley by 1750. During the early nineteenth century the family exchanged their holdings for real estate elsewhere in the city. The children's letters chronicle events of national importance as well as daily domestic life. Reading them now, from our perspective of nearly 150 years, conveys a poignant taste of the joys and sorrows of their lives and gives us as adults a chance to see Jacksonian America through the eyes of urban children.

Anthony N. B. Garvan

Introduction

In late December 1834 Quaker Jacob Elfreth gave his children a blank book, or diary, in the hope that they would use the book to "improve in . . . writing and keep memorandums of passing events." Elfreth's wishes were indeed fulfilled, for *The Elfreth Book of Letters* contains over one hundred letters written by five members of the Elfreth family between 1835 and 1837. While journals, or "commonplace books," were frequently used during this period for recording daily events as well as contemporary prose and verse, what sets the *Book of Letters* apart from other examples of this genre is the number of diarists who created the book, and, more significantly, the ages of the principal diarists. As the book begins in January, or "first month," 1835, the Elfreth children are all less than ten years old: Joseph, the eldest, is nine; Jane, seven; Caleb, six; and Sarah Elfreth, four. The *Book of Letters,* quite simply, is the first collection of letters written by nineteenth-century Quaker children to come to light.

The children's entries are complemented by letters written by their father, and the "conversations" that take place between the children and Elfreth clearly illustrate the revolutionary changes in attitudes toward children that occurred only shortly before the *Book of Letters* was written. Although adults recognized the physical and intellectual limitations of children, the idea of children requiring special nurturing and protection did not exist before the seventeenth century. Since the concept of children as a discrete group having different, yet acceptable forms of behavior was unknown to adults, it comes as no surprise that children participated in most aspects of adult life, and "had seen and heard it all." For generations, in short, children and adults inhabited the same social and intellectual worlds.

The dramatic scientific, intellectual, and economic changes associated with the Enlightenment, however, profoundly altered the way adulthood, and thus childhood, was perceived. The development of the printing press and the subsequent increase in literacy contributed heavily to this change, as adults who were able to read were now viewed and treated differently than those who could not. Children, of course, fell into the latter category, and the educational needs of children created by this turn of events prompted the first appearance of juvenile literature suited to the specific abilities of children.

Not surprisingly, the earliest works written for children in the American colonies were religious in nature. In New England children were constantly reminded that they were not "born to live, but born to dye," and were admonished to prepare for the "Hell of Eternal Fire" or the "Blackness of Darkness Forever"; these were only a few of the horrors awaiting those who did not achieve salvation, which was by no means guaranteed to even the most well-behaved child. Only one hundred years before the *Book of Letters* was written, children were described by Massachusetts clergymen as "a meer nest, root, fountain of sin and wickedness" whose hearts were "unspeakably wicked." The experiences of American children, however, differed widely throughout the colonies, and Quaker spokesmen used remarkably softer language when proscribing religious and moral advice for children. William Penn, for example, urged his children to "fear God and avoid that which is Evil and do that which is good." Dublin Quaker Samuel Fuller's catechism, printed in the early eighteenth century, advised parents to foster "good and early impressions on tender minds" and encouraged those charged with the care of children to "watch over them for good, maintaining our authority in love."

The malleable, or "tender," nature of children's minds and the innocence of childhood were dual concepts that grew throughout the eighteenth century. These unique characteristics of children required new methods of teaching, and learning, it was believed, should be made play and recreation. Illustrated books such as *The Child's New Plaything: Being a Spelling-Book Intending to Make the Learning to Read a Diversion Instead of a Task* was printed in Boston in 1750, and the first edition of *Mother Goose Nursery Rhymes* appeared in England just six years earlier. The emergence of juvenile literature expressing these new attitudes paralleled changes occurring in the home as well. Walking stools that prevented children from engaging in the animal-like practice of crawling were used less often toward the end of the eighteenth century, and loose frocks that permitted greater freedom of movement replaced earlier tight, restrictive clothing worn by children. Not surprisingly, specialized playthings for children now appeared in staggering varieties and quantities. "1559 dozen children's watches," "592 paper toys," "17 gross, 7 dozen pewter toys," "6135 string beads," and "97 tin chairs and coaches" were only a fraction of the playthings stocked by a Philadelphia "Toyman" in the early 1800s. The doll tea set and "small box of paints" given to Jane Elfreth following a painful trip to the dentist and the toys included in her 1837 Christmas list were thus easily and inexpensively provided by local merchants.

Although the types of toys used by children nearly two hundred years ago are strikingly similar to many enjoyed today, the Elfreth children's letters suggest that different forms of play and recreation were enjoyed by children when the *Book of Letters* was written. Taking trips with their father to visit relatives in New Jersey was a favorite pastime of the Elfreth children, particularly when the journey involved walking across the frozen Delaware. The children often spent part of the summer months with relatives in the Jersey countryside, as noted by Joseph's longing for the pleasure of visiting his uncle's farm where he could "run about and ride in the cart and help the boys." And like many nineteenth-century Philadelphians, the Elfreths enjoyed long walks to Laurel Hill cemetery and "Fair Mount," located several miles west of the family's home. Trips to the museum were also enjoyed by the children, and Jane accompanied her father to anatomy lectures in 1837.

In addition to revealing much about the changing role of children as reflected in contemporary literature, artifacts, and child-rearing practices, the *Book of Letters* provides a wealth of information about one of childhood's most influential experiences—primary education. As indicated by the forms of recreation enjoyed by the family, learning during this period was not confined to classroom hours but was expected to continue through appropriate use of leisure time. Thus walks were taken not simply for the benefit of physical exercise, but to broaden one's understanding of the natural and built environments. That children were catalysts of their own educational experiences was a widely accepted belief, for it was "inconceivable how many things children would learn, were we but careful to improve all the opportunities which they themselves supply us." Elfreth's letters poignantly reflect this view, for he often uses subjects of particular interest to his children as vehicles to supplement their classroom experiences.

Just as the content of Elfreth's letters can be considered representative of contemporary educational practices, the form he chose as his medium is equally significant. Letters performed several important functions for eighteenth- and nineteenth-century correspondents. As a form of communication, the letter, of course, is historically rooted in the epistolary tradition and fulfilled both personal and didactic purposes. It comes as no surprise that Benjamin Franklin recommended the use of letter-writing as an educational tool for young students, and his words uncannily describe Elfreth's methods used in the *Book of Letters* almost one hundred years later:

> *To form their style, they should be put to writing letters to each other, making abstracts of what they read, or writing the same things in their own words, telling or writing stories lately read, in their own expressions.*

As the concept of childhood as a preparative period for adulthood grew, letters assumed greater significance for middle-class Americans: well-written, properly composed letters were regarded as evidence of good manners and good breeding. An instructional book on letter-writing entitled *An American Letter-Writer* was printed in Philadelphia in 1793, and numerous manner books produced during the nineteenth century include the topic.

While the form and content of Elfreth's letters can be considered representative of popular beliefs concerning learning as a continuous, ongoing process, his words also reflect distinctly Quaker attitudes toward education. Although early Friends did not encourage higher learning for members, they were strong advocates of providing educational opportunities for their children. The acquisition of "useful knowledge" was emphasized, and suggested curriculum included the study of Greek, Latin, arithmetic, and geography. Both boys and girls were encouraged to improve themselves through learning, and girls who attended the Westtown School founded by Friends in 1799 were taught the same subjects as boys in addition to classes in needlework. It is interesting to note that fanciful, or "make-believe," tales were not copied into the *Book of Letters*, for they were considered "untruthful" by Quakers. Although the fairy tales that appeared toward the end of the eighteenth century were heralded by many as being suitable for children, others believed, as Elfreth probably did, that children were best served by reading lively, amusing stories centered around realistic characters and plausible events. Elfreth's gift of a copy of "Peter Parley's Magazine" to Joseph in 1835 supports this view, for the author of these very popular tales, Samuel Goodrich, describes the Parley stories as "designed to be both instructive and amusing, with the narrative form used as an agreeable medium by which knowledge and virtue might be imparted." Books for children, like toys, were available in abundant quantities during this period; more than 100,000 copies of the Parley tales were sold in 1832 alone.

The education of children during the early nineteenth century, however, was not limited to such subjects as arithmetic, geography, and history. Religious precepts and moral values were considered equally important components of a child's education, and this is clearly illustrated throughout the *Book of Letters*. The Elfreths were members of the Northern District Monthly Meeting in Philadelphia and remained Orthodox Quakers after the Hicksite schism, or "Great Separation," of 1827; Orthodox Quakers championed early, traditional Quaker tenets and rejected the Hicksite, or Liberal, Quakers' emphasis on mystical revelation and greater tolerance of diversity. Elfreth's frequent use of biblical references reflects distinctly Quaker characteristics, and scriptural verse is dutifully copied by the children throughout the *Book of Letters*. Despite the religious tone of sections of the book, however, the theme that emerges most clearly in the *Book of Letters* is secular rather than religious in nature: "To be good is to be happy" recurs throughout the lessons imparted by Elfreth and his wife to their children. This notion is a frequent theme of books written for children at this time and also appears in books containing advice for parents that emerged during the nineteenth century. Thus while the *Book of Letters* reflects Quaker devotion to educating children and contains distinctly Quaker characteristics, the diary also represents the increasingly secular world in which the Elfreths lived.

The *Book of Letters* thus reflects the specialized role assigned children during this period, early educational practices, and distinctly Quaker traits. On another, more immediate level, however, the letter book clearly communicates the love and affection the children and their parents feel for one another. The children's father applied the popularly held view of the period that "reason and tenderness will do more with children than the iron hand of correction." Although Elfreth initially assumes a stern, disciplinary tone when denying Joseph's request to visit his cousins in New Jersey, he ultimately allows his son to make the trip. Similarly, when Joseph leaves home for the first time to attend school at Westtown, Elfreth continues to write letters to his absent child, wistfully noting, "I often think about thee, and look forward to the time of thy coming home." He enjoyed spending time with all of the children, whether it be watching "a splendid view of the Aurora Borealis" with them, helping Jane wind skeins of yarn, or preparing cabbage for pickling with the help of the children. A bookkeeper by profession, Elfreth enjoyed keeping records of family activities and was a firm believer in the value of "keeping memorandums of passing events." In addition to his contributions to the *Book of Letters,* he kept a separate diary and recorded verse he enjoyed, conversations with friends, and newspaper clippings; his separate "memorandums" fill no less than forty-five volumes.

While it is clear that Elfreth found the *Book of Letters* a pleasurable and perhaps relaxing way of spending time in the evenings, his feelings were not unanimously shared by the children. Jane, for example, apparently regarded using the book as something of a chore, for her entries often include relieved notes that she "was done writing for now" or comments such as "you wanted me to write a little verse, and so I did," suggesting an occasional unwillingness to use the letter book. The letters by Jane and Joseph are the most interesting of the children's entries, for the two oldest children were able to write the lengthiest and most descriptive letters. Elfreth often gave the children assignments to complete by writing in the *Book of Letters,* and it is when the children depart from this form that their letters come alive. Jane's description of a painful trip to the dentist cannot fail to evoke sympathy, but readers are cheered by news of gifts presented by her parents as rewards for being a good patient. Joseph's letter describing fire engines seen while out on an errand conveys every child's fascination with these machines, and he notes that his father, too, would have enjoyed seeing them. Many letters written by the children evoke images of domestic scenes of the day, such as taking tea with grandparents in the nursery and Elfreth busily cooking apples in the family kitchen. Through the children's letters, the *Book of Letters* tells us much about the everyday activities of a middle-class family living in Philadelphia during this period.

When the Elfreths began the *Book of Letters* in 1835, the family consisted of the four children who appear in the diary, their parents, and servant girl Elizabeth Chaloner. Although Jacob was the great-great-grandson of Jeremiah Elfreth, who gave Elfreth's Alley in Old City its name, the family never lived on the alley but instead made their home nearby in the Northern Liberties section of the city. Shortly after his marriage to Abigail Pierce in 1821, Elfreth bought a five-room house at No. 15 Wood Street, located between Vine and Callowhill above Fourth Street. The family moved several blocks west to No. 84 Wood Street in 1830 and lived here throughout the completion of *Book of Letters.* The Elfreths probably moved to this house to accommodate their growing family, for five more children were born to Jacob and Abigail. Jane, Joseph, Caleb, and Sarah, all survived their parents, and news of how they spent their adulthoods is contained in the Afterword found at the conclusion of the diary.

Despite plans of moving to the country in 1840, Jacob Elfreth and his wife remained in Philadelphia. Abigail was a strong woman who remained very close to her father, hardware merchant Caleb Pierce, after her marriage to Elfreth; her parents may not have initially approved of the match, for Jacob notes that he and Abigail had a "long and difficult courtship." Mr. Pierce was instrumental in dissuading Jacob from moving the family to the country, and his daughter vowed she would "not lift a finger" to carry out her husband's plan. After her husband died, Abigail and five of her nine children, who now ranged in age from their early thirties to mid-fifties, moved outside of the city where they shared quarters in Darby Borough. In her will she notes that "all my children are equally dear to me," but she nevertheless made special arrangements for the support of her three unmarried daughters, Sarah, Rebecca, and Mary. Abigail is described as having "unselfish devotion to her fellows"; she died in December 1881.

Jacob Roberts Elfreth was employed as a bookkeeper by Richard Oakford from 1817 to 1839, and makes several references to his work in the *Book of Letters*. He was not happy with his situation, and after leaving Oakford's firm in 1839 hoped he could successfully earn a living "without again coming under bondage to any man in the way I have been for the last twenty-two years." Born in 1789, Elfreth was one of the earliest students at the Westtown School and taught at Westtown in 1814. He was an avid book collector and assembled an interesting working library that included Homer's *Iliad*, Quaker works such as Clarkson's *Portraitures* and *Barclay's Apology*, biographies of Benjamin Franklin and Patrick Henry, Wollstonecraft's *A Vindication of the Rights of Woman*, history books, and poetry; he also collected coins, sea shells, and autographs of friends and students. After leaving Oakford's employ, Elfreth found work as a book-keeper with the Lehigh Navigation Company in 1840 and remained with the firm until shortly before his death in 1870. He complained bitterly about the eight hundred dollars he earned annually in 1840, and his financial situation improved but little over the years. His estate was valued at four thousand dollars when he died, and an inventory of his household contents indicates a modestly furnished home, including a small amount of silver, "9 spoons and 1 can."

The amount of personal belongings left by Jacob Elfreth, however, is of little consequence. For by entrusting the *Book of Letters* to family members who lovingly cared for what appeared to be an odd and amusing copybook over the years, he has indeed left a gift of great value. Although portraits or silhouettes of the diarists remain undiscovered, *The Elfreth Book of Letters* paints a more complex and interesting portrait of a Philadelphia family and the times in which they lived than could be captured on paper or canvas. *Book of Letters'* survival, in fact, is one of the most unique aspects of the diary, and suggests when contemplating a cluttered attic or dusty box of family papers—tread lightly.

SOURCES

Aries, Phillippe. *Centuries of Childhood*. New York: Vintage Press, 1962.

Braithwaite, William C. *The Second Period of Quakerism*. London: Macmillan, 1919.

Elfreth Diary. The Quaker Collection. Haverford College, Haverford, Pa.

Goodrich, Samuel. *Peter Parley's Tales About the State and City of New York.* New York: 1832.

Heininger, Mary Lynn Stevens. *A Century of Childhood, 1820–1920.* Rochester, N.Y.: The Margaret Woodbury Strong Museum, 1984.

Hinshaw, William Wade. *Encyclopedia of American Quaker Genealogy.* Ann Arbor, Mich.: Edwards Brothers, 1938.

Kiefer, Monica. *American Children Through Their Books, 1700–1835.* Philadelphia, Pa.: University of Pennsylvania Press, 1948.

Postman, Neil. *The Disappearance of Childhood.* New York, N.Y.: Laurel Books, 1982.

Rosenbach, A. S. W. *Early American Children's Books.* Portland, Maine: Dover Books, 1933.

Welch, D'Alte. *A Bibliography of American Children's Books Printed Before 1821.* Boston: American Antiquarian Society, 1972.

Elfreth wills and administrations are available at the Delaware County, Pa., Register of Wills; Philadelphia County Register of Wills; and the Camden County, N.J., Surrogate Court.

*The
Elfreth
Book
of
Letters*

Philadelphia 1mo 1. 1835

My Dear Mother

Father has bought this book for us to write in that we may improve in our writing and keep memorandums of passing events. On the twenty third of last month our next door neighbour Thomas Myers died, and on the twenty eighth of the same month his little son Thomas died. he was about eight years old and went to school to John Weaver where I have been going for some time past in vine street below sixth street on the South side. I went to see the corpse and so did my sisters Jane and Sarah and my brother Caleb. He was buried on the thirty first of this 12 month 1834. Cousin Isaiah Everett has returned from New York on the 27 of Twelfth month.

thy affectionate son

Joseph R Everett

Philada 1 mo 2º 1835.

Dear Father
                I have never written a
letter before this — How does thee do
this evening is thee well and hearty
like me — If I lived in the country
I would "At early dawn arise, and
see the rising sun, and view the
pearly dew, and feed the gray
chickens, the geese and the goslings —
On the 1st day of the 1st month 1835
my cousin Samuel D Elfreth was
married to Martha Scroggy. he
is a Blacksmith and he lives
at Camden near the river Del
aware in the state of New Jersey.
I should like to go over the river
and see him — will thee to
take me one of these days —
farewell for this time and take
care of my letter — Caleb P Elfreth

24

Philadᵃ 1 mo 5ᵗʰ 1835

Dear Jane

I think it would be better for
thee if thee had a little more useful em
ployment than thee seems to have – Thee
might dust off the chairs and settee in
the nursery. and put things to rights,
and beat up thy bolster in the morning –

Thee sometimes helps to dress thy sister
Sarah and thy brother James, but is apt
to get out of patience and seems to think
it is a hardship, whereas thee ought to
be willing to help thy Mother who
has a great deal too much to do –

I have heard thy Grandmother say
thy mother used to iron when she was
so little that she had to stand on a
stool to reach up to the table – Now
my dear little Jane do try. to be more
industrious and make thyself useful –

I am thy affectionate father

Jacob R Elfreth

Philad.ª 1 mo 6th 1835

Dear Children

It is better to guard against danger, than to be frightened when it overtakes us— Caroline Fry in the "Listner" says "In respect to the fear of accidents and injuries from our fellow Creatures, I believe the best cure for it is an abiding sense of the ever present Providence of God: and if we are Constitutionally timid, we cannot better subdue it than by cultivating this consciousness of the Divine protection, in such a manner that it may recur to our minds on the first movement of alarm. In short so as to become influential on our habits and sensations, and make a part of all our thoughts and feelings"—

Wishing you may possess courage without rashness, and Caution without timidity I am your affectionate father

Jacob R Elfreth —

26

Philadelphia 1 mo 8th 1835

Dear Father

The weather is very cold and has been so for a week nearly. this morning the thermometer was 7½ degrees above zero. the river Delaware is frozen over and a great many people have been on it, walking and skating and it is likely in a few days people will hall wood over it on sleds. At Albany it has been a great deal colder than it is here. the thermometer there was 32 degrees below zero. last second day we moved the cast iron stove out of the parlour into the nursery because the stove we had there would not keep us warm. yesterday grand father and grand mother were here and took tea with us in the nursery. Several hogs were frozen to death in the streets a few nights ago in the city of New York. The snow at the city of Washington has been two feet and a half deep but there has not been much here this winter.

I am thy affectionate daughter
Jane P Elfreth.

Philad^a 1 mo 10 – 1835

Dear Salley
            This day we got a new
Stove in the parlour it is a large
sheet iron stove with a clay Cilinder
it was bought of William Taylor
in 2^d Street and Cost eleven dollars
besides one dollar and a quarter
for the pipes – he allowed us $3
for the old stove that used to
be in the nursery –

This afternoon Grand father and
I walked across the river Delaware
on the ice, it seemed very solid and
firm; we saw a great many people
sliding and skeiting we also saw
many sleighs drawn by horses
and two boats fastened together
drawn by a horse on the ice
                I am thy affectionate
    brother   Joseph R Elfreth

28

Philad{o} 1 mo 11th 1835

Dear Brother James

Thee cant read my letter
now but perhaps thee will be able to
some years hence if thee learns to write
Cousin Hannah Elfreth dined with
us to day and after dinner she and
Father and brother Joseph and myself
walked across the river Delaware
on the ice and went to see Cousin
Samuel D Elfreth and his new wife
we drank a glass of wine with them
and after staying abut an hour
walked across the river again: we saw
a great many sleighs and horses and
the river and one sleigh and two
horses broke in through the ice but
they were got out again Joseph
slid upon the ice, and fell down
several times but was not hurt
            Thy affectionate sister
            Jane P Elfreth.

Philad 1m 12 – 1835

Dear Mother

I think thee must be
very tired this evening as thee has
been helping Susan Brown wash to day
Last seventh day evening a little
boy was drowned in the river Schuylkill
he broke through the ice and his Fath
who was with him also got into the
water but was dragged out by F C
Jones, Thos I Firth and another man
who laid down on the ice and threw
him one end of a coat to which he
held on until they pulled him on
to the froen ice —

Cousin Josiah Elfreth drank tea
with us this evening and is going
to sleep with me in the 3^d Story
room fronting the South — Little James
is on the Settee —

Thy affectionate son
Joseph R Elfreth

Philad^a 1 month 13th 1833

Dear Sally,

The weather yesterday and to day has moderated very much. The Thermometr this morning was 34 degrees above zero and the ice and snow in the streets has melted very fast. The people still continue to walk across the river Delaware. my uncle and aunt Ezra and Phebe Haines walked across it to day and are now at Grand Fathers.

This Evening William Burrough, Isaac Davis and two women friends paid us a visit in the parlour. Father and Mother and Joseph and Myself were there. Caleb and thyself and dear little James had gone to bed.

Our Dear Mother has been very poorly these several days with a severe pain in her face. gideon brown has been cleaning away the ice in our alley this afternoon it was so filled up that the walter could not run down to the end of it. I am done writing now.

I am thy affectionate sister
Jane P. Crowth

Philadelphia 1/15 1835

Dear Uncle Samuel

Thee came to town today
and we were glad to have thy company
at super and I hope thee will lodge with
me to night. Thee brought us a nice
little pig, and Father a letter from
cousin David. together with two of
cines of lime stone and a collection
of shells dug out of the hill side near
Mumington Creek, for all which we
are much obliged to thee, I should
be glad if I was going home with
thee for I love to beat your house where
I can run about and ride in the
cart and help the boys work,
but I cannot go with thee this
time but I hope I shall go next
summer if nothing happens to prevent
Iam thy affectionate Nephew
Joseph R E Elfreth 1835

Love each other

Little children love each other ~~is the blessed savio~~

  Is the blessed saviours rule

Evry little one is brother ~~to his~~

  To his playfelow at school

We're all children of one Father

  The great God whoe reigns above.

Shall we quarrel? No much rather

  Would we be like him all love.

He has placed us here together.

That we may be good and kind

He who's stronger then his brother

  Let him be the weak ones friend —

Who's more playthings than his brother

  He delights to give and lend

Selfish children sad behaviour

  Shew they love themselves alone

But the children of the saviour

  Will not call the best their own

All they have they share with others

  Give kind and gentle words

    Jane P Elfreth 1 m 16th 1835

Philada. 1 mo 17 – 1835

Dear Father

The Laws of the United
States are executed by the President
assisted by the Secretaries of State,
of War, of the Navy and of the
Treasury; and is called the Executive
Power. — The President of the U.S.
is chosen for 4 years, by delegates elected
for that purpose by the People, and are
equal in number for each State
to the members its sends to Congress
The Vice President, who is President
of the Senate, is elected for the same
number of years and in the same
manner — The Senate consists of
2 members from each State chosen
by the Legislatures thereof, for 6
years — The Representatives are
chosen for 2 years by the People
of each State, according to their

population. 47,700 inhabitants being entitled to One Representative. —

The Federal Judiciary is the power which explanes and applies the Laws and is independent of the Legislature. It consists of a Supreme court held at Washington and a District court held in each State. — The Judges of the Supreme court of the United States and the inferior Officers of Government are appointed by the President with the approbation of the Senate.

Thus the Ambassadors to foreign Countries Consuls Collectors of Revenue, Governors of the Territories Land agents Paymasters of the army, & &c are appointed by the Presidents and confirmed or rejected by the Senate. —

The Generals of the Army & Captains of the Navy are appointed by the President who is Commander in chief. —

Philadª 1 mo 19th 1835

Dear Brother Caleb

The following is a
List of all the Presidents of the
United States I dont expect thee
will ever be President but it
is well to know who have been
George Washington from 1789 to 1797 = 8
John Adams   „ 1797 to 1801 = 4
Thos. Jefferson   „ 1801 to 1809 =
James Madison   „ 1809 to 1817 = 8
James Monroe   „ 1817 to 1825 = 8
John Quincy Adams „ 1825 to 1829 = 4
Andrew Jackson   „ 1829 to

George Washington, Jas Madison
Thomas Jefferson and James Monroe
were born in Virginia —
John Adams and John Q Adams
in Massachusetts — Andrew
Jackson was born in Sth Carolina —

Philada / mo 21–1835

Dear Mother

Our friend Elizabeth Edwards
dined with us yesterday – and in
the evening thee went to see our
neighbours Pemberton, and Henry Pem=
berton spent the evening here with
father – The Brig George Gardner
is at the marine rail way wharf
below Catharine street, she is
frozen up in the ice, but is taking
in her cargo for Valparaiso – the
following is a part of it – 186 pigs
of Lead weighing 22005^{lb} cost 3¾ cts per ^{lb}
100 bags Coffee 12.225   „ – 9¾ „ „
47 bags Pepper 5135   „ 7¼ „ „
150 barrels Tar cost $2.00 per bbl
75 „ Pitch   „ 2.25 „ „
25 dn ball back Chairs at $11.00 per dn
25 „ bent   „ — ditto „ 9.00 „ „
26 „ straight „ — ditto „ 8.00 „ „

37

Philad 1 mo 22 1835 —

Dear Father

This afternoon thee took
me to Daniel Neak in Arch Street
above 3 a dentist whoe extracted
two teeth which were decayed —
It hurt me considerably but it
it was soon over and I was
very glad when it was over
and came home much happier
than I went — This afternoon
Mother gave me a set of Cups
and Saucers, a Slop bowl, Sugar
bowl, cream cup & Tea pot
and thee brought me home a
small box of paints — So I am
very well pleased that my
troublesome teeth are out and
that I have received in exchange
for them such aceptable presents
Thy affectionate daughter
Jane P Elfreth —

38

Philad.ª 1 m. 24th 1835

Dear Children

You love to hear about ships, so I am going to tell you about a brig, which three of you have seen and been on board of — The Brig George Gardner stands A N°.1, which means a first vessel, or one of the highest class It was built in Baltimore in 1824, is 104 feet 6 inches Long, and 27 feet 3 inches Broad — Burthen by measurement 344 Tons + $\frac{55}{95}$ and will carry upwards of 4000 barrels of Flour — The last voyage was from Baltimore 8 mo 10 — 1833 thence to to Richmond to take in Flour — She went to sea 8 m 29 and arrived at Valparaiso on the West coast of South America 12 m 7 — 1833 from there she went to Lima and to Cobija and Copiapo, and took in a cargo of Copper Ore 354 Tons weight which is 892,960 pounds — She then sailed to Swansea in Wales where she arrived 8 m 5 — 1834 then went to New Port & took in a cargo of Rail road Iron 356 Tons sailed from there 9 m 21 and arrived at Philad.ª 11 m 11 — 1834 —

Farewell to you J R E° —

Philada 1 M 26 - 1835

Dear Joseph

The brig George Gardner is nearly ready to go to Sea again - Beside the articles mentioned under date 21st inst she has now on board 1300 bbls wheat Flour, 10000 feet Lumber 15 bales Cloves which cost 20 cents for lb 25 bbls Beef which cost $7 50/100 and 40 bbls Mess Beef cost $12.00 - 20 bbls Prime Salt Pork Cost $1200 75 bbls Rosin cost $1.62½ per bbl The Flour cost $5.12½ per barrel Besides the above there was a bale of Cotton Drillings 6000 yds cost 11 cts 10 bales of Russia Sheetings at $750 per piece and Several cases of Silk Pongee Handkerchiefs — 500 boxes Canton Crackers 2 cases fine light Prints 500 kegs of Gunpowder &c &c

Thy affectionate Sister
Jane P Elfreth

Philad.ª 2 mo 2ª 1835

Dear Children

      The brig George Gardner left
the wharf last 4th day afternoon with her
Crew on board viz (she cleared next day 1m 29th)
John Henry Smith, Master at $60 = pr month
George S.t Lownes 1st Mate at 35 = „   „
Joseph Harvey Jr. 2d mate at 20 „   „
a Carpenter . . . . at 18 „ —„
a Cook . . . . at 14 „ —„
a Steward . . . . . at 14 „ —„
8 Seamen . . . . at 14 „ —„
2 Boys . . . . at 7 „ —„
In all sixteen persons at an expense of
$287.00 per month besides their provisions —
She was cleared at the Custom House the
next day and carries with her a Permit
signed by Andrew Jackson President of
the United States which is to serve for
her protection in all parts of the world —
So now we will let her rest for a while
        Your Father J R Elphett

Philad 2m 3d 1834

Dear Joseph

"Sic transit gloria mundi". Thus
passes away the glory of this world —
As I was walking with thee a few
days since in Coates street above John st.
I pointed out a persons name on the
door of a small two story house —
when I came to this city in the year
1817 this man was supposed to be
very wealthy but he was pleasant
and affable in his manners as I had
an opportunity of witnessing more
than once — at one time I think about
the year 1826 he owned 4 large
ships viz The "Addison", "Woodrop Sims,
"William Savery" and "Thomas Scattergood"
which were all engaged in bringing
Teas from Canton — but suddenly
his riches departed from him, and
he became an inhabitant of Arch
street prison where I saw him — His

son who was the American Consul at Canton was obliged to leave there on account of ill health, and died just after he reached home — She who in the days of his prosperity was the wife of his bosom, has separated herself from him in the day of adversity — and I have been told he now lives without any family except a coloured man who is in the capacity of a domestic — and yet if he has a conscience void of offence toward God and man, his present situation may be happier than when he was surrounded by all the luxuries that money could command, but harassed with the cares and perplexities of business which made his pillow instead of being one of peaceful repose, a pillow of vexation and of thorns — "Sic transit gloria mundi" — remember that —

"Thy father J R E —

Philad⟨ª⟩ 2ᵗ mo 6ᵗʰ 1835

Dear Father

   Cousin Mary Deny
Was at our house to day and Dined
with us. Mother went out to
Grand Fathers and staid to Diner
and to Tea ⟨?⟩ yesterday Brother ⟨?⟩ Joseph
is a writing his lesson and I Ruled his
Papers for him. My lipip is very soar
Thee said thee would give me some
Mouth Watter. Little James is
asleep and so is Caleb and Sister
Sarah. Brother James is in our little
Bed. he used to Sleep in the Nurcery
but he does not now. Lisabeth is a
reading a Chapter in the Testament
and now she is Just done. Mother
made a little shirt for Brother James
this Morning. Cousin Mary deny
had thy spectacles. Thy affectionate
te Daughter Jane ⟨?⟩ Epeth.

Philad⁹ 2 mo 6 1835

Dear Brother James

I would be glad if the
was as big as Caleb then thee
could sleep up stairs with me
I have been writing my lesson
and have just got done. The Brig
George Gardner left the wharf
Yesterday a week with her crew viz.

John Henry Smith master at $60=7ᵐᵒⁿᵗʰ
Geo S. Doms 1ˢᵗ mate at 35 " "
Joseph Harvey 2 mate at 20 " "
a Carpenter .... at 18 " "
a Cook .... at 14 " "
a Steward .... at 14 " "
8 Seamen .... at 14 " → "
2 boys .... at 7 " → "

So I hope the will have a good
nights sleep.—

and so farewell for to night
this Thy affectionate brother
Joseph R. Elbreth

24

Philad.ᵃ 2 mm 8ᵗʰ 1835

Dear Joseph.

The brig George Gardner took
for Provisions for the Captain & Crew
2 Hhds & 20 bbls Pilot Bread 2691 ℔ 4½ᶜˢ ℔ 121.09
22 Hhds & 2 bbls Navy Bread 9415 ℔ 3¼ 305.99
Cost of 24 Hhds a 1⁵⁰ & 22 bbls a 75ᶜ Emptys 3.00 55.50
                    Cost of Bread   482.58
40 bbls Mess Beef a ℔ 12.00 .... 480.00
20 bbls Prime Pork a 12.00 .... 240.00
Groceries & Small Stores Tea Coffee &c _____
                    Together
Estimate of Provisions for ones month viz -
450 ℔ Beef a 6ᶜˢ is ℔ 27.00
112½ ℔ Pork a 6ᶜˢ .. 6.75
675 ℔ Bread a 4ᶜˢ .. 27.00
100 ℔ Flour a 3ᶜˢ 3.00
Groceries .... 16.68 .. ℔ 80.43
This is Calculated for 15 Persons —
a Barrel of Beef Contains 202 pounds of Beef
a Barrel of Flour Contains 196 pounds —
The Thermometer this morning was at 3½° above zero —

Philad 2 mo 9th: 1835

Son Joseph   Thee observed the other day
as we were walking together, that if the brig
George Gardner should take fire at sea and be
burnt up with all her Cargo, it would be a
heavy Loss to Richard Oakford — This was a
reasonable conclusion for thee to come to, but it
was not a true one — If the brig was to be
burnt, or if she was to sink with all her cargo,
He would lose nothing by it except a little
interest perhaps, because they are insured —
Prudent people may insure their Property
both at Sea and on land against fire, and
all other accidents likely to happen to it
at sea, Such as Shipwreck, foundering or
Sinking, Capture by pirates, or by ships of war
&c and this is done by paying a Small
Sum of money to a Company of men who
make it their business and their interest to
insure other peoples property from Such loss —
This may appear Strange to thee but I will
try to explain it to thee — Suppose there are

one hundred Ships insured by this Company
and each Ship is worth $10,000 =, the value
of the whole would be $1,000,000 =. The
Insurance Company would insure them all
against loss for one year for 3 per cent or
$3 = for every $100 = (per cent means per hundred)
This is called the Premium of Insurance –
well then, the Premium that the Company
would receive on the 100 ships would amount
to $30,000 =.... Now suppose two of them
Ships should be lost at Sea during the
year, the Insurance Company would have
to pay the owners of them $20,000 = But
then they could afford to do so, because
they had received $30,000 = for insuring all
of them, and so they would gain $10,000 =,
for if we Subtract $20,000 from $30,000 –,
$10,000 = would be left ——
In the same way we can Insure Houses
and Merchandise on land against Loss
by Fire + This does not cost so much as

to insured ships at Seas, because the risk or danger
is not so great — a merchant may Insure $20,000 =
on his goods in Store against Fire, for a quarter
of one per cent, or 25 Cents on every 100 dollars —
this would cost him but $50 = per year, and
Surely it is much better for him to pay $50 =
than to run the risk of having $20,000 = worth
of goods destroyed by Fire — If he thinks
that in Case of fire half of his goods might
be got safely out of the Stores, he may
insure but $10,000 = for which he would only
have to pay $25 per year — I get $800 insured
on Household furniture of every description,
wearing apparel, (Clothes,) and books in use
for $2 = per year — and the house No 15 Wood
Street is permanently insured for $1200 = by
my paying at one time about $30 = I dont
recollect the exact sum, as it has been
several years since I got the Insurance
effected — if I had had it done yearly it
would have cost me $3 = per year —

So farewell for to night — Thy Father JRE

Philadel 2 mo 13th 1835

Dear Father

The Eastern States
are six in number, viz. Maine,
New Hampshire, Vermont, Massa-
chusetts, Connecticut And Rhode-
Island. Maine extends farthest East
it also extends farthest North.
Connecticut extends farthest South
Maine is the largest of the Eastern States.
Rhode Island is smallest of the Eastern States
Vermont has no sea coast. All the other
Eastern States have sea coasts. Vermont
New Hampshire and Maine are
bounded on the North by Lower
Canada. Vermont Massachusetts
and Connecticut are bounded West
by New York. Massachusetts is the
most populous of the Eastern
States Thy Son
Joseph R Egbert

50

Philadelphia 2 mo 14 – 1835

Dear Brothers & Sister

We each of us have a box in which we keep our money. This evening when you were, all absent I counted it and will tell you how much there is in each box —

In Joseph's box there is 88 cents
In James   "   "   "   16½
In Caleb's "   "   "   14½ "
In Sarah's "   "   "   14   "
In Jane's   "   "   "   8   "

altogether 141½ cents or one dollar and forty one cents & a half — Joseph has gone with Mother to Grandfathers and all the rest of you have gone to bed — Last fifth day evening Father and Joseph and I went to the Pennsylvania Institution for the Deaf and Dumb to see Cousin Hannah Elfreth

From Your Sister Jane P Elfreth

Philad.ᵃ 2 m̅ᵒ 10ᵗʰ 1835

Dear Jane

As thee appears to be interested
in Geological Specimens more than thy
brothers or Sister I will give thee the
result of an analysis of a portion of
Lime Stone from Mannington hill — 50 parts
of Lime stone yielded 27 parts of pure
Lime and 23 parts of Sand and earthy
matter — This is equal to 54 per cent of
Pure Lime — Geology is derived from
two Greek words Γε the earth and Λογος a
discourse — which means a discourse about
the Earth — Analysis, is a separation of
parts to discover their proportions — Thee
was with me when I was analysing the
Lime Stone and I dare say thee remembers
the process — Thee may read this to
thy uncle Samuel Allen when he
comes to see us as he has a large
quantity of Lime stone at home —
              Thy father J R Elphetts —

52

Philad 2 mo 17 1855

Dear Mother

On the 15th of this month
I finished reading the Bible, and last
evening I began to read the Reference
Bible edited by Harvey Wilbur — It is
moe than two years since I began to
read the Bible through —

Yesterday morning the pavements
were covered with a sheet of ice —
it hailed and rained the proceeding
night and froze as it fell — a great
many boys were skating on the pave-
ment yesterday and the walking
was very slippery — I fell down as
I was going to school but did not
hurt myself much — James Murdoch
moved into the House next dor to us
yesterday, when neighbour Meyers
fumerly lived —

I am thy affectionate Son
Josiah R. Ellwoth

32

Philad. 2 m 19. th 1835

Son Joseph

This day I paid Jno Weaver's Bill for thy Schooling — the following is a copy of it —

Jacob R. Elfreth

To John Weaver Dr

1834		
12 m 20	1 Copy Book &c	12½
1835		
1 m 20	1 do	12½
2 m 12	1 do	12½
" 18	1 Quarter Tuition pens & ink for Joseph	4. 25
		$4. 62½

Since thee began to go to School, I have paid a good deal of money for thyself and thy brother & sister — perhaps if I were to tell thee how much, thee would be more careful to improve thy time than thee has been, so I will make a Statement of it on the next page — Thy Father
J R E

54

1828
9 m 12 p⁰ Mary Hillman for 1 D: Tuition Joseph 7 day, $2.00
1829
1 m 10 p⁰ do   do   " 12 D: do   ditto   " 2.25
9 m 24 p⁰ Jesse Stanley   " 15 weeks do   ditto ... 5.51
10 m 24 p⁰ do   do   " Tuition of do ditto .. 4.00
1830
6 m 1 p⁰ Mary Hillman   " 1 D: do   ditto .. 3.00
10 m 18 p⁰ do   do   " 1 D: do   ditto 3.00
1831
1 m 18 p⁰ do   do   " 1 D: do   ditto 5.45
5 m p⁰ do   do   " 1 D: do   ditto 4.52
" 28 p⁰ Sarah Elfreth   " James board & Schooling 5.00
7 m 16 p⁰ do   do   " ditto   " ——— .—— 5.00
9 m 5 p⁰ Mary Hillman   " 1 D: tuition Joseph 4.58
12 m 7 p⁰ do   do   1 D: tuition Joseph & Jane 9.25
1832
3 m 7 p⁰ do   do   1 D: " Joseph 4.94
4 m 2 p⁰ Mary White 1 D: " Jane 3.00
6 m 6 p⁰ Mary Hillman 1 D: " Joseph ... 4.50
7 m 3 p⁰ Mary White 1 D: " Jane 2.50
12 m 5 p⁰ Thomas Branson 1 D: " Joseph 5.56
" 26 p⁰ Maria Pearson 1 D: " Jane & Caleb 4.13
1833
3 m 28 p⁰ Thomas Branson 1 D: " Joseph 4.71
7 m 27 p⁰ George McGlauer 1 D: " ditto 4.40
" 29 p⁰ Lydia Reeve 1 D: " Jane & Caleb 8.25
Carried Over leaf $95.55

1833   Amount brought forward $95.55

11 m 26 p?   L & B Reeve   12r.   Tuition Jane & Caleb   9.25
   1834
1 m 24 p?   Geo M Glover   12r.   ditto Joseph   4.50
2 m 17 p?   L & B Reeve   1 2r.   do Jane   4.13
4 m 16 p?   Geo M Glover   1 2r.   do Joseph   5.50
8 m 2 p?   John Weaver   ½ 2r.   do   ditto   2.25
" 26 p?   L & B Reeve   1 2r.   do Jane & Caleb   8.25
11 m 19 p?   do   do   1 2r.   do   do & do   8.63
" 26 p?   John Weaver   1 2r.   do   Joseph   4.62
   1835
1 m 19 p?   do   do   1 2r.   do   ditto   4.62

           Together $147.30

Besides which I have pd more than $10.00 for
books most of which were for thee —
By the above it appears I have paid
upwards of $84.00 dollars for thy Schooling
and I think thee has made but a poor
return for it indeed — So I advise thee
to double thy diligence for, it will be
time for thee before long to go apprentice
and get thy living by thy Labour —
"He that will not work should not eat" —

56

Philad" 2 mo 22 1835

Dear James

On the 30th of 1 month
1835 an attempt was made to
assassinate Andrew Jackson
President of the United States,
by a young man named Richard
Lawrence, while he was attending
the funeral of Warren R Davis a
member of Congress. He snapped
two pistols at him and although
the percussion caps exploded neith
of the pistols which were loaded with
powder and ball went off. He was
about four feet from the President
and pointed the pistols at his breast
He was secured immediately, examined
before a Judge and committed to
prison. Two respectable Physicians
have seen him in prison and
pronounced him to be insane.

Thy brother S R Elfreth

Philadelphia 2 mo 22 1835

Dear Mother &

This is the birth day of
the great George Washington who was
born in Virginia 2 mo 22°. 1732 —
He was the Commander in chief
of the armies of the United States
during the Revolutionary war
and was afterwards elected the
first President of the U S and
continued in that high Station
from 1789 to 1797 during which
time he lived in Philadelphia
in Market Street a few doors
below 6th Street — He afterwards
retired to his Farm at Mount
Vernon on the river Potomac
where he died 12 mo 14th 1799
after an illness of 23 hours
He was a great and good man —

Thy affectionate Daughter
Jane P Elfreth

On sitting down at meals
When at my meals I take my seat,
  My thoughts to heaven I raise;
That I may favoured be to eat,
  With gratitude and praise.
This grateful sense of bounteous good,
  Such humble feelings spread;
That while I eat my outward food.
  My soul has heav'nly bread.

Philadelphia 2 mo 25th 18

Dear Father

          The wanted me to write
a little else and so I did. The ship
Sully arrived at New York last
week from France which brought
news of a pacific nature. Before
she arrived it was expected there
would be a war with France
          Thy affectionate daughter
I am   D Elfreth

Peptic Apophthegms —

To miss a meal sometimes is good
It purifies and thins the blood;
Gives nature time to clean her streets
From filth and crudities of meats. —

Let supper little be and light,
But none, makes often the best night,
Gives sweetest sleep without a dream,
And morning mouth sweet moist & clean.—

After dinner, rest awhile, —
After supper, walk a mile —

If you be living and wish to be dead
Eat a cold apple on going to bed—

Philad^a. 3 mo 6 — 1835

Dear Grandfather

The Lot on which the Alms House is situated, between 10th and 11th, and Spruce and Pine Streets, was sold last week for $140,000. — The purchaser afterwards sold it, it is said for $180,000 —

The ship Washington got on the Alceste rock in the Straits of Gaspar on the 2d of 11 mo 1834 — It is expected the ship and cargo will be entirely lost — and perhaps all the poor sailors will be killed by the Malay Pirates who infest these parts —

We have had a very cold winter, but the weather has been mild to day with the wind at N.E. —

Thy affectionate granddaughter
Jane P. Corlies

61

Philad.a 3 mo 16 th 183

Dear Father

On the 11th of this month
my dear little sister was born she
is a nice plump little girl and
we are all very fond of her —
I have held her in my arms 11
times and Caleb and Sally and
James have all had her in their
laps, — Mother is quite brave and
I hope she will be about again soon
Caleb is staying at Grand Father
and Jane went to Haddonfield
last 6th day afternoon. — Cousins
David and Jeremiah Allen took
tea with us on the 13th of this mo
The kitchen chimney took fire this
morning it ought to have been
swept. — I have been splitting wood
this evening and am tired
so farewell thy son
Joseph R Elfrett

62

Philad^a 3 mo 17 — 1835

Dear Joseph

Thee has heard some talk
about the probability of a war with France —
While Napoleon Bonaparte was Emperor of that
Country a great deal of American property
was unjustly seized by the French; and since
his death our Ministers at the Court of
France have been trying to get payment
for this property — at last the present king
of France, Louis Philip (who was once a
poor Schoolmaster in America, and knew how
hard it was to have his property taken from
him) agreed to pay the Americans a
large Sum of money 25,000,000 francs which
is about $5,000,000 — A Treaty was made to
that effect and was signed at Paris
7 mo 4th 1831 — The money was to be paid in
6 instalments together with interest from 2 mo 2d 183?
at which time the Treaty was ratified at Washington — But the French Chamber of Deputies

would not agree to pay the money — on the 6th
of 4 mo 1833 the Bill to make the appropriation
was submitted to them, and they rejected it
in the 4th month 1834 which was nearly 3 years
after the Treaty was made — Our President
Andrew Jackson was very much offended
at such bad treatment on the part of
France, and when Congress met 12 m 1 1834
in his annual message he complained of
their not fulfilling the Treaty and wanted
Congress to give him the power of seizing
upon French Property in this country if
France would not pay the money — But
Congress would not consent to that —
When the French king heard how our
President had been scolding he became
angry too and sent a ship of War to
this country with a message to the French
Minister residing at Washington to come
home — But I am in hopes the French
will pay the money & we shall not
have war — Thy father J R Elliott

Philad.ª 11 mo 17ᵗʰ 1835

Dear Mother

Thee weather is a little colder than it was. I hope thee will be better to morrow than the was to day so the can set up. I went down to Ruth Jesses to day and got Grandmother bonet to day. The things do not look so well as thay do when the is about thee things do not look so bright either I hope the will soon get well anough to tend to them. Elizabeth does a great better than when Jane is at home I would be glad to see her and Sarah too and James too. I broke a pitcher to night.

So farewell thy son

J R E Greete

Philada 3 mo 18th/ 1833

Dear Farther.

Please to show me how to do this sum.

A Captain, mate, and three seamen, having recaptured their vessel, estimated at 5240 dollars, were to receive from her owners, ⅕ of her value in cash; allowing the captain 3 shares, the mate 2, and each seaman 1 share how much is the part of each?

The whole value of the vessel is $5240 =

The Crew are to receive one fifth of this

Then $5240 ÷ 5 = 1048$ Sum to be divided

$1048 is to be divided into 8 shares

$1048 ÷ 8 = 131$ amount of 1 share

The Captain has 3 shares.. $131 \times 3 = 393$

The Mate has 2 shares.. $131 \times 2 = 262$

Each Seaman has 1 share $131 \times 1 = 131$

Answer Capt $393 = Mate $262 = Each Seaman $131 =

Philad. 3 mo 17th 1835

Dear Father

I would be glad if
thee would let me go with Uncle
Samuel home cousin Hannah and
me could have so much fun we
could play about and cousin Han
nah and me could go a fishing and
take walks together. Mother is
better to day than she was yesterday
she talks of setting up tomorrow
maybe Sister Rebecca Ann will
be better than she was yesterday
or to day and set in my lap to
morrow that was a very sudden
case of Joseph Marshel master
said he saw him the other day
and said he looked a ~~hearty~~ heuty as
ever Sally wrote in my spelling
book today

thy son

I R E

Philad^a 3 m 14th 1835

Son Joseph

I have read thy letter, and if I
was sure thee would be a good boy, and
not to be troublesome to thy uncle & aunts
but would be better there than thee is at
home I should be willing thee shoulds go
to Manincyten if thy uncle Samuel is
willing to take thee — I shall be pleased
if thy mother is well enough to sit up
tomorrow; and hope thy little sister Abigail
will be well enough for thee to nurse her
which thee seems very willing to do — she
is a nice plump little body and is one
week old — The weather has been cool
and blustring yesterday and to day — last
night there was a good deal of rain
with the wind from N.E. but to day the
wind has been Westerly — Joseph C Marshall
died 3 m 16 he had not been in good health
for some years — Thy affectionate father
J R Elbret

An Italian Song

Dear is my little native land   vale
The ring dove builds and murmurs   warbles there
Close by my cot she tells her tale
To every passing villager
The squirrel leaps from tree to tree
And shells his nut at liberty.

In orange groves and myrtle bowers
That breathe a gale of fragance round
I charm the fairy footed hours
With my love lutes romantic sound
Or crowns of living laurel weave
For those that win the race at eve.

The sheperds horn at break of day
The ballet danced in twilight glade
The canzonet and roundelay
Sung in the silent greenwood shade
The simple joys that never fail
Shall bind me to my native vail

Auxilliary = helper, assistant.

Avenue = an entrance.

Avidity = an Eagerness.

Award = to give judgment.

Awful = solemn venerable.

Awkward = clumsy.

Awry = unevenly.

Axis = a line that passes through any thing on which it turns.

Azure = blue.   **B**

Bachelor = A man unmarried.

Backbite = to censure or reproach the absent

Badge = a mark or token

Baffle = to elude confound balk

Bail = a surety for another.

Baize = a coarse cloth.

Balsam = an Ointment.

Ballast = weight to ballance a ship

Balmy = soothing soft healing

Baneful = poisonous destructive

Banish = to send or drive away

Banner — an ensign
Banquet — a feast
Barbarity — cruelty
Barrenness — unfruitfulness
Barrier — a defence
Barter — to change one thing for another
Bashful — modes shy
Basis — the ground work

Philada 3 mo 24 1835

Dear Father

at thy request I have written my lesson. This day I attended Monthly meeting for the first time. It was held in New Street between Front and Second streets. It held till near two o clock. The bill to light the City of Philadelphia with Gas passed the Councils on the 21st Instant.   Thy son

Philad^a 3 mo 26th 1835

Dear Father

Last Year an iron
Pallisade fence upon a foundation of
hewn stone was placed on the South
and East sides of Franklin Square
which cost several 1000 dollars, and
its is expected the fence will be
made on the North and West sides
this year. Last evening thee wrote
a letter to Cousin Mary S t ffrett
in reply to one received from her dated
the 10 of this month at Clermont board
ing school where she has been
for some time past. I want to
see sister Jane perhaps she will
send me a letter next seventh
day as I wrote one to her last
seventh day and sent it by Aaron
the Haddonfield stage driver
thy son
J R E

Philad.ᵃ 3 mo 26ᵗʰ 1835

Dear Father

Thee sent me a errond this evening it was very pleasant running it is always ~~in~~ pleasant walking in Arch Street. I went an errond for Mother and bought some cakes for her. it is very warm to day especially in the sun I which the engines would not make such a noise and the bell to. ther is a engine in the city of Philadelphia that is the prettiest ever I saw her wheels were all brightened and she is a very nice one. when I saw her she was in the street she stands in Chery street between sixt street and fith street I which thee had been with ~~y~~ me then the could saw her too.

thy son

J R E⁄

Philadelph⁴ᵃ 4 mo 1ˢᵗ 1835-

Dear Dear Father

I have a very hard
lesson to lern to night. on the
29ᵗʰ of last month thee took Caleb and
me to Haddonfield to see Aunt Sarah
and Aunt Elizabeth and Sister Jane
who has been there the last two
weeks. We Returned home the same
day. Yesterday thee bought a cord of
Hickory wood for $6.06 Cartage 67 and
a half cts and sawing 81,2 5 cts I have
been pilling it to day but have not
got quite done there are a great
many shad in market thee bought
one last seventh day for 37 and a
half cent. it was a one and
we had the eggs fried for breakfast
last second morning

thy son
Joseph R E

Philad.ª 4 month 2.ᵈ 1835

Dear Father

This day we had a visit from
Dugald Clark and his wife Aseneth Clark.
Aseneth Clark is an approved minister
of the Religious Society of Friends. She is
a daughter of Nathan Hunt of North
Carolina. She had a private sitting
in mothers room and spoke comfortably
to her, When she was going away she
bid me farewell and told me to
be a good boy which advice I hope
I shall attend to.

The bought two shad to
day for 25 cents each they were fine
large ones and weighed 9½ pounds.
I went to the store after dinner
and brought them home, It has
been warm to day, and thundered
and lightened this evening but did
not rain,

Thy son J R E

Philadelphia 4th mo 14th

Dear Father,

since I rote in this book I have been spending four weeks at Haddonfield with my Aunts Sarah and Elizabeth. I went there on the 15th of 3^d month and returned home on the 6th of this month – I had a pleasant visit there and came home fatter and better than I went – My brother Caleb has been at Grandfathers since the 12th of last month – To day thee bought him a new pair of shoes at Clark & Conovers they cost 75 cts Mother moved into the Nursery yesterday, but she is very poorly & hardly able to keep about – Nurse went away last 6th day evening – Next week will be Yearly meeting perhaps brother Joseph will go over to Haddonfield in a day or two – Fare well thy daughter Jane P Elfreth

Philad. 5 mo 1 1835

Dear Children

This morning Wm Everhart of
West Chester was at our store and bought
3 Rolls of Matting — He is remarkable as
being the only passenger who was saved
when the Ship Albion was wrecked on the
Coast of Ireland 4 mo 21st 1822 = 22 of the
Passengers and 24 of the Ships Crew were
drowned only 8 of the sailors being saved —
You may read an interesting account
of this melancholy Shipwreck written
by Wm Everhart in the 27th number of
the "Friend" vol 8 = date 4 mo 11 — 1835 —
He is a plain clever looking man and
is said to have made a great deal of
money lately by the rise of property in
the town of West Chester where he
resides — Few men have been so near
death to all human appearance as he
was and yet to survive it —

Your Father J R Elfreth

56.

Philad^a 5 m 7 1835

Dear Jane

Thy brother Caleb and thee
began again yesterday to go to school to
Lydia & Beulah Reeve in 4th street
above Callowhill street — I bought a
new geography for thee to day & desire
thee will take good care of it, and
try to improve in thy learning, for thee
may not always enjoy the privileges thee
now does — There are many little girls
in the world who never go to school,
and have not even an opportunity
of hearing other people read to them —
How sorrowful it is that these
poor children should be brought up
in such ignorance — Many of them
are also taught to worship images
or idols made of wood and stone
instead of the true God who made
them and all of us —

Philada 9m 14th 1835

Dear Children

It has been several months since
I wrote you a letter in this book — now let
me tell you a few things which have taken
place since — On the 30th of 5 month Sally
went to Haddonfield to go to School to her
aunt Sarah — She returned home 8 mo 14th —
Caleb was very ill on the evening of 6 mo 1
I took Jane to Middletown 6 mo 6th, we
went with Enoch Yarnall in his dearborn
waggon; paid a very pleasant visit at
Uncle John Mendenhalls, and returned
home 6 mo 8th by the West Town Stage —
On the 15th of 7 month I entered Joseph
to go to West Town School I expect he
he will go some time in the 10th month —
He quit going to School to John Weaver
about the 6th of the 8th month, since then
he has been to his uncle Samuel Allen
where he staid about three weeks —
Mother and Jane have paid a visit to

uncle John Mendenhalls, and Jane staid
there several weeks — Poor Caley has not
been out of town this summer I believe
which is a hard case as all the rest
of you have been so much or so long —
On the 7th of this month Caleb and
Sarah, and Elizabeth Chaloner began to
go to School to Mary Hillman — a day
or two after, Jane also began to go in
the afternoons to take Elizabeth Chaloners
place who is only to go in the mornings
as Mother cannot spare her all day —
Elizabeth Lord began to live with us
5 mo 5th and staid until 9 mo 5th.
Since then we have had a colored
woman named Alice Berry who is the
sister of James Gooseberrys wife — her
husband lives in Maryland and is a
slave — She has several children who are
slaves in Maryland, and two children
who are free in this City ——

Your Cousin Josiah Elfreth has been very
ill at Haddonfield with billious fever;
he has been almost entirely confined to
his bed more than five weeks, but now
seems to be slowly on the recovery & I was
to see him on first day & returned by the
stage in the evening — Your Cousin Samuel
Allen Junr. began to teach School at the
Orange Street School house 8 month 24th
he boards with Deborah Swain in 7th St.
next door to your Grandfathers, his brother
David Came up with him on the 22d of
last month, and spent a few days with
us very acceptably — His Uncle Jedediah
Allen and Jedediah Allen Jr. were to see
us last week — the latter went with
Joseph to the Museums, to Fair mount &c —
Cousin Hannah Elfreth has been to Hart-
ford in Connecticut, she returned home
very poorly, but is better than she
was, and I hope she will soon be well —
Your affectte father J R E

Philad. 9 m 15. 1835

Dear Children

This day my employer
Richard Oakford removed from N? 84
Market Street — It was a great trial to
me to leave this pleasant Country home
and Store where I have been located for
more than ten years; but I hope also
to find our present place of business
an agreeable one — it is on the other
side of Market Street, N? 87; and is
the 3ᵈ house above the Commercial
Bank — R. O. is to have the 2ᵈ 3ᵈ & 4ᵗʰ
Storys, and the use of the Cellar for
$500 = a year — The House was built
by Joseph Crukshank to whom it belongs —
G B & J B English occupy the lower
Story as a Silk Store — Joseph helped
us Move and was very useful — Richard
Oakford made him a present of a
large bundle of Canton Pattern Cards —

Philad.ᵃ 11 mo 15ᵗʰ 1835

Dear Children. Jane Caleb & Sarah —

Your brother Joseph went to West Town
Boarding School 10 mo 17ᵗʰ 1835 — He went in the stage,
I did not go with him, as we thought it would
be better for him to go alone, and for me to pay
him a visit the latter end of this month, as it
cost no more than if I went with him; and would
be pleasant to see him after he had been gone
a few weeks — It was a trial to him to leave
home but he went away like a man without
crying any — I hope he will be a good boy,
and then he will be happy and it will
be a comfort to his father and mother —

He has written letters to us every fourth day
since he went, and also several times to his
Grandfather and his Aunts Anne and Rebecca —
I sent him a quart of Chesnuts yesterday &
a volume of Parleys Magazine both of which
I expect will be very acceptable to him —

The day before yesterday we received three

barrels of Apples from your uncle Samuel Allen
to whom we are much obliged for such a
useful and acceptable present — I received
a letter from cousin David Allen at the same
time — Your uncle Samuel has been a long
journey this fall. He attended the Yearly
meeting of Indianna and afterwards went
through the state of Ohio from West to East —
He reached home safely about two weeks ago
but is not in as good health as he was
before he went —

Samuel L. Walter removed from N.º 15 Wood St.
last 6th day the 13th of this month — he
has been living there about 11 months, and has
paid his Rent up to 9 mo 3d. —

We have heard of the arrival of the
brig George Gardner at Valparaiso. They
had a very boisterous time in going round
Cape Horn, and two of the sailors left the
brig at Valparaiso. She is going from the
West Coast of South America to Calcutta —

Your father J R E

Philad^a 11 mo 15 1835

Dear Mother

I was at meeting to
day and heard two friends preach
One of them said "Thou hast been
faithful in a few things I will
make thee ruler over more.—

The other said, thou shalt love
the Lord thy God with all thy
heart and with all thy mind
and with all thy strength,
and thou shalt love thy
neighbour as thyself. On these
two Commandments hang all
the Law and the Prophets."—

The names of the two friends
were Hannah Mitchell and
Thomas Smith. Don't thee think
I improve in my writing?

Thy little son
Caleb P Elfreth

Philad. 11 m, 22 1835

Dear Grandmother

I should like to see
thee very well and how is Rebecca
Bacon Peirce and Grandfather and
aunt Anne and is the girl pretty
well – and we have had a holiday
this day and Sarah is writing a
litter to Joseph and I have wrote
me also – I would like to see you
all and I would like to see
cousin Hannah and Joseph –
It is Snowing to day a d it
melts as fast as it falls down
None of the boys at our School
knew their lessons yesterday but
I intend to learn my lessons
and try to be a good boy –
Aunt Sarah is in town and
she brought us a bag of apples
I am thy likely grandson
Caleb P Elfreth

Philada 11 mo 25 1835

Dear Aunt Sarah

I heard thee was sick
and I hope thee will be well.
and come to see us tomorrow.
I hope Aunt Mary Allen
will come to see us too and
that you will both be here
together

I am thy little niece
Sarah Elfreth Junr.

A. B. C. D. E. F. G. H. I.

J. K. L. M. N. O. P. Q. R. S.

T. U. V. W. X. Y. Z. &.

a. b. c. d. e. f. g. h. i. j. k. l. m.
n. o. p. q. r. s. t. u. v. w. x. y. z.

66.

Philad.ª 12 mm 6ᵗʰ. 1835

Dear Children

On the first day of this month I
went to West Town in the stages to see your
brother Joseph and found him well & happy –
I staid there until the 3ª inst. and had
a very pleasant visit – Joseph and I took
several rambles over the hills and along
the Canal – the Farm house and the mill,
in the garden and through the woods –
at the Mill Joseph weighed 78 pounds; a
little while before he went to West Town
he weighed only 70 pounds – I made my
home at Cousin Cyrus Mendenhalls, they
were very kind to me, and also to Joseph
who took his meals there with me –
West Town is a fine healthy place. The
Farm contains 600 acres and cost $16000. =
There are about 250 Schollars there now
during the year ending 2 m 28ᵗʰ 1835 the
average number of Boys were 119 and of Girls
115.   Your Cousin Jacob R. Elliott

The African Mother.

Help! O help thou God of Christians!
　　Save a mother from despair.
Cruel white-men steal my children:
　　God of Christians! hear my prayer.
From my arms by force they rend them,
　　Sailors drag them to the sea;
Yonder ship at anchor riding,
　　Swift will carry them away.
There my son lies pale and bleeding,
　　Fast with thongs his hands are bound,
See the tyrants how they scourge him,
　　See his sides a recking wound.
See his little sister by him,
　　Quaking, trembling, how she lies
Drops of blood her face besprinkle,
　　Tears of anguish fill her eyes:
Now they tear her brother from her,
　　Down below the deck he's thrown,
Stiff with beating, through fear silent,
　　Save a single death-like groan.

Hear the little sister begging,
    Take me white-men for your own;
Spare! oh spare my darling brother,
    He's my mother's only son.
See upon the shore she's raving,
    Down she falls upon the sands,
Now she tears her flesh with madness,
    Now she prays with lifted hands.
I am young, and strong and hardy,
    He's a sick and feeble boy;
Take me whip me chain me starve me
    All my life I'll toil with joy.
Christians! who's the God you worship?
    Is he cruel, fierce, or good?
Does he take delight in mercy,
    Or in spilling human blood?
Ah! my poor distracted mother
    Hear her scream upon the shore —
Down the savage Captain struck her,
    Lifeless on the vessel's floor.
Up his sails he quickly hoisted,
    To the ocean bent his way,

Headlong plung'd the raving mother
From an high rock, into the sea. —

_____

Philad^a 12 mo 27th 1835

Dear Children

You have heard of the <u>Great
Fire in New York</u>: It broke out about 9 o'clock
in the evening 12 mo 16th. 1835 and burnt till the
afternoon of the next day. The weather was
extremely cold, and a high North west wind
caused the fire to burn rapidly, there was
not a good supply of water as there is in
Philadelphia, or the fire perhaps might have
been stopped sooner than it was; Seventeen
blocks of buildings of the most costly description
were destroyed including the Exchange in which
was the Post Office: 670 buildings have been burnt,
principally occupied as Stores by Importers and
whole sale merchants — The buildings were estimated
to have cost $3,000,000 — and the Goods destroyed
were supposed to amount to $15,000,000 — It is

supposed that including the streets, the Fire
extended over an area of 50 acres — nearly
the whole section bounded by Wall street,
Broad Street and Coenties Slip was burnt—
down to the East River — At first it was
thought all the Insurance offices would be
insolvent, but it is now believed most of
them will be able to pay in full or
nearly so. The Bank of the United States
has liberally offered to discount Bonds for them
to the amount of $2,000,000 and it is expected
the City of New York will create Stock to
the amount of $10,000,000 to loan to Merchants
who are Sufferers by the fire, application
has also been made to Congress who will
probably extend the Credit on their Bonds
for duties to a period of several years or
perhaps cancel them — As most of the
Sufferers by the fire resided with their
families in other places there was not
so much personal suffering as there would
have been if the fire had broken out

in some other quarters of the City –

Though this was the greatest Fire there
has ever been in the United States, it was
small in extent compared with the Great
Fire in London which broke out in the night
of September 2. 1666 and burnt for nearly five
days, destroying 13,200 houses and 89 churches
covering 373 acres within the City walls, and
63 acres without the walls – In the fields
were seen lying on the bare ground or under
huts hastily erected 200,000 individuals,
many of them in a state of utter desti-
tution, and others watching the small
remnants of their property which had been
saved from the flames – If you wish
to see further particulars of those terrible
Calamities, see the Saturday evening Post
of 12 mo 26th and the Philada. Gazette
of the same date and other Philadelphia
newspapers from the 18th to the 26th of 12 month –

　　　　Your affectionate father,
　　　　Jacob R Elfreth

The little Straw platter.

Here I sit and plait the straw,
  All the livelong day ma'm!
Neater never lady saw,
  So I'm sure you'll say ma'm.
'Tis an on and on concern,
  Nothing very sprightly;
Yet our daily bread I earn,
  And take my Mother nightly.
Much I thank the lady fair,
  Who has had me taught it;
Once I us'd to romp and tear,
  'Twas not I who sought it.
Then in rags I us'd to go,
  I have a sickly Mother
I could neither knit nor sew;
  Only nurse my Brother.
Now my Brother runs alone
  Able just to totter,
Oft my Mother had to groan
  'Till her meals I brought her.

How it cheer'd her languid eye
When my gairy I brought her,
Oft I hear her sighing say
"Bless thee my good daughter".—

Copy of a Letter from Mother
12 mo 29th 1835

My dear little Sarah

I am happy to receive a letter from thee and hear that thee is well. I hope thee will soon be able to write plainer and that I shall have more time to answer thy letters. I love to see thee enjoy thyself playing, and I want thee to enjoy thyself _working_ too _sometimes_. I love thee very dearly and want thee to be good and happy

Thy affectionate
Mother

To
S Elfreth Junr.

Copy of a Letter from Mother

Phila. 12 mo 99 - 1835

My dear little Caly

Thy letter was
very acceptable and I often
regret that I have not more
time to devote to my little
ones in a literary way. I
should love very much to receive
a letter from each of you every
day and answer them too. and
I want thee to try all thee can
to learn so that thee may
write long interesting letters.
and be a good scholar as thee
tells me thee has spelled that
far in thy spelling book, and
and try to be better than wise;
and never tell a story on any
account, for it is very wicked; and
as thy sister Sarah told James this

morning "thee Lord will not excuse
thee" I very often think about thee
when thee is asleep, and desire that
if thee should grow to be a man
thee may be a good one. I have
not time to write any more.

Affectionately thy mother
A P Elfreth

Copy of a letter from Mother
Philada 12 month 29th 1835

Dear Jane

Thy letter gave me much
pleasure, and I am glad thee has
such a fancy for thy pen; but always
remember that whatever is worth
doing at all, is worth doing well:
but we can do nothing well without
attention. and also dear, cultivate
a happy temper — Never allow thyself
to fret and whine. It is disagreeable
to every body, and the older thee
grows

the harder it will be to overcome
it — Remember the old saying, "a
cheerful countenance betokens a
good heart". — I want thee to be
happy in thyself and a comfort
to others — with love affectionately
thy mother
Abigail P Elfreth

Philada 1mo 11th 1836

Dear Grandfather
The sun shone out to
day for the first time since the 2nd
day of this month — during the
eight days of cloudy weather we
have had a great deal of rain
and snow and a part of the
time the wind was North East
but during the last three days
it was North West — The snow
was so drifted and deep yesterday

that Jonathan Davidson our milk
man did not bring us any and
we had to drink our tea without
milk but Mother put a little
more sugar in it than usual

Caleb and I have been to school
to day, I got my feet wet, and
Sarah Hillman was so kind that
she gave me a pair of dry stockings
to put on — Aunt Elizabeth Elfreth
has been in town paying a visit
but she had an uncomfortable
time as regard the weather and
did not go any where but here
and to Cousin Roberts — She went
home to day sooner than she expected
having heard that Aunt Sarah
had fallen and hurt herself
very much — With love to you all
    I am thy affectionate granddaughter
      Jane P Elfreth.

Philadᵃ 1 mo 14 1836

Dear Father

My little brother
James has been very poorly,
and Mother gave him some
medicine and soaked his
feet this evening.—
            Thy little daughter
                Sarah Elfreth Jr.

A solitary blessing few can find —
Our joys with those we love are interthind
And he whose watchful tenderness removes
                                    he loves
the obstructing thorn which wounds the friend
Smooths not anothers rugged path alone
But scatters roses to adorn his own — ..

Mem. made 5 m 29 1836. Last evening I heard
Elizabeth Redman had set into on her journey to the
States, accompanied by her sister Beulah Hopkins
and Samuel Nicholson — I feel much concern for them

The Tabby Cat.

One Summers day, some boys at play
   Espied a Tabby Cat,
Who from her home, had chanc'd to roam
   In search, of mouse or rat.
The boys were rude and would intrude
   On Tabbys liberty;
The day was hot, and puss had got
   Beneath a shady tree.
Says Tom to John, "Let's set Tray on,
   And hunt the Cat away."
"Aye, that we will" says naughty Bill,
   And called aloud for Tray.
The dog he ran and soon began
   To worry the poor Cat;
When Ann and Jane came down the lane
   To see what they were at. —
The dog ran fast, but puss at last.
   Climb'd up into the tree —
The Boys were sad, the Girls were glad,
   Puss had her liberty .

                    P. T. O.

80.

"Let's pelt her down," said little Brown,
    And pick'd up a great stone
Jane beg'd and prayed, Ann cried & said
    Do let poor puss alone –
Jane's tears prevailed; Brown's courage failed
    The stone he did not throw –
The Boys called Tray to come away,
    That Puss in peace might go. –

———————

                    Philada 1 mo 17th 1836
Dear Brother James

        There is a great deal of
snow on the ground, and the sleighs
bells have been ringing merily –
I have seen ninety four sleighs
to day – One of our little Schollars
died last evening or this morning,
with the scarlet fever his name
was George Williams –
    Thy affectionate sister
        Jane P. Elfreth

Philad. 1 mo 20 1836

Dear Father

The President of the U.S.
Andrew Jackson sent a message to
Congress on the subject of the differ
ences with France on the 19th of
this month which is not of so
pacific a nature as it was hoped
it would be, and it is now feared,
by many, that there will be a
war before the business is settled,
as it ought to have been long ago.—
France has acted very badly
in refusing so long to pay a debt
which she had acknowledged to be
due to the United States.— see
some account this business under
date 3 mo 17th 1835.— But little
girls like me had better learn
to knit stockings than to be talking
about politics   Thy daughter
                        Jane P Elbeth

A foolish son is the Callamety of his Father 5 87

Silver . . . . The Idols of the Heeathens were Silver and Gold . 587.

If thow be wise thow shall be wise for thyself. 977. . . . Wisdom dwell with Prudence and find out Knoledge. 977

A merry hart maketh a cheerfule contenance. 976.

A faithfull witness will not lie 971

A wicked messenger falleth into mischief. 976. A wise Man is strong yea a Man of knoledge knowledge increaseth strength 916

Lull'd in the countless chambers of the brain
Our thoughts are link'd by many a hidden chain
Awake but one, and lo! what myriads rise!
Each stamps its image as the other flies.
Pleas of Memo. p. 95

Philad 1 mo. 28th 1836

Dear James

Thee has been reading this evening about the number of the Children of Israel when they were in the Wilderness of Sinai, on the first day of the 2nd Month, in the Second year after they were come out of the land of Egypt. Numbus 1 chapter by which it appears that there were men of 20 years old and upwards able to go forth to war as follows.

Children of Reub	46,500	Simeon	59,300
Gad	45,650	Judah	74,600
Issachar	54,400	Zebulon	57,400
Ephraim	40,500	Manasseh	32,200
Benjamin	35,400	Dan	62,700
Asher	41,500	Naphtali	53,400
			263,950

Together . . 603,550

The tribe or family of Levi was not included in the above, so that we may suppose if they had been counted

and all the women and children too,
the whole number would amount to
nearly or quite two millions of people
who were fed in a miraculous manner
with bread from heaven, in the wilderness.
and we are also told that their
clothes waxed not old upon them forty
years Deut VIII.4. But in consequence of their
unbelief all of the 603550 men perished
in the wilderness except two, namely Caleb
and Joshua who were permitted to enter into
the promised land. "The Lord brought his
people Israel out of the land of Egypt
from the house of bondage; he led them
through the great and terrible wilderness
wherein were fiery serpents and scorpions
and droughts, where there was no water,
and he brought them forth water out of
the rock of flint; he brought streams also
out of the rock, and caused waters to run
down like rivers — He rained down manna

upon them to eat, and gave them of the corn
of heaven. Man did eat Angels food. He
rained flesh also upon them as dust, and
feathered fowls like as the sand of the sea.
He found them in a desert land, and in
the waste howling wilderness; he led them
about, he instructed them, he kept them
as the apple of his eye. As an eagle stirreth
up her nest, fluttereth over her young, spreadeth
abroad her wings, taketh them, beareth them
on her wings; so the Lord alone did lead
them, and there was no strange god with
him. — But, "they forsook God who made
them, and lightly esteemed the Rock of
their salvation. They sacrificed unto devils,
not unto God." — In the book of Deuteronomy
thee may read a very interesting account of
the children of Israel, which it is believed
was written by Moses the Man of God, during
the last two months of his life. See also Psalm LXXVIII

Affectionately thy father
Jacob R Elfreth

86.

Philad. 2m. 3. 1836

My dear little Sally,

I received thy letter last
evening, and I am pleased to find thee
likes to write to thy Mother and me —

The weather has been very cold of late—
the river Delaware is frozen over and the
people walk across it on the ice—perhaps
they will haul wood across it tomorrow
on sleds. — The thermometer yesterday morning
was 2 degrees above zero, and this morning it
was 4 degrees — It is overcast this evening
with light clouds and perhaps we may
have snow to night — There is a great deal
of snow on the ground now, and the side
walks are coated with ice so that the
walking is very slippery — Many persons
have had falls, and some have had
their arms or legs broken — Thy Aunt
Rebecca B Peirce is very poorly and has
not been down stairs these two days — Thy
Mother and I were to see her this evening

She is very patient, and bears her sufferings
without complaining, and I desire that thee
and I and all of us may follow her example
when we are laid on the bed of sickness
for it would make it much easier to our-
selves and to those about us, than if we
were fretful and complaining — Last third
day week was our Monthly meeting day,
and Joseph Snowden and Hannah Ecroyd
appeared and declared their intentions of
marriage with each other — A very goodly
old fashioned friend named Christopher Healy
was at our meeting last first day, and
also at our Quarterly meeting the day before
yesterday, has preached to us and told us
many good things which I hope may be
useful to some — This is the fourth day
of the week I went to market in High
street this morning and bought some beef
and parsnips, some horse radish and carrots —
          Thy affectionate father
                    Jacob R Elfreth

88

Philad. 2 mn 7th 1836

Dear Caleb

This morning I walked across
the river Delaware on the ice, and
rode in a Sleigh to Haddonfield to
see thy aunt Sarah who is confined
to her bed in consequence of a fall
which happened 4 weeks ago from yesterday—
as she was attempting to stand up in
a chair to do something to the clock,
the chair slipped from under her and
she fell with violence on the floor—
I returned home this afternoon through
a snow storm and walked across the
river on the ice— there were a great
many persons on the ice, some sliding
some skating, some walking, & others
riding in sleighs— one of the sleighs had
painted on its side "Crochet — go ahead"
and it went ahead very swiftly —
            Thy affectionate father
                Jacob R. Elfreth

Philadᵃ 2 mo 15ᵗʰ 1836

Dear Joseph.

As thee is now a school boy at
West Town, it is not likely thee will read this
letter before the middle of 4 month next, about
which time we expect thee will pay us a visit

After a long time of apprehension that
our happy Country would be involved in a
war with France, we this day received the
pleasing intelligence that the Presidents message
at the opening of Congress in the 12 month last
had given general satisfaction in France, and
that they are prepared to pay the money
in dispute together with interest thereon from
the time it was due – Thee may see some
account of the origin of this difficulty between
the nations in a letter to thee in this book
dated 3 mo 17ᵗʰ 1835 – I often think about thee
and look forward to the time of thy coming
home with a great deal of satisfaction
                        Thy affectionate father
                            Jacob R Elfreth

90   Philada. 3 nov 7th 1836

Dear Jane
          The Charter of the Bank of the
United States expired on the 3d. insta. that is
on the 3d day of this month and the next
day the New Bank of the United States
went into operation in this city under a
Charter from the State of Pennsylvania,
with a Capital of $35,000,000 - This Bank
has to pay a large sum for its Charter
almost four millions and a half of dollars -
Two millions of which are to go to the School
fund so that all the poor children in the
State may have Schooling, and the rest is
to be laid out in Rail roads turnpikes &
So that I am in hopes the State of Penna
of which thee is a native and I am not,
will be benefitted by the Bank - I am
not very well this evening, so for this time
farewell - I have received thy two letters
              Thy well wisher and father
                    Jacob R Elfreth

Lo, the poor Indian! whose untutor'd mind
Sees God in clouds, or hears him in the wind;
His soul proud science never taught to stray
Far as the solar walk, or milky way:
Yet simple nature to his hope has given,
Behind the cloud-topt hill an humbler heaven,
Some safer world, in depth of woods embrac'd,
Some happier island in the watery waste,
Where slaves once more their native land behold,
No fiends torment no Christians thirst for gold.—
To be; Contents his natural desire—
He asks no angel's wing, no Seraph's fire,
But thinks admitted to that equal sky,
His faithful dog shall bear him company.—

    The above was written by Alexander
Pope one of the finest poets of England.—
it may be found in his "Essay on Man",
a beautiful poem, but in some parts
tinctured with fatalism, and supposed
to have been sketched by Bolingbroke.—

Philad. 5 m 29. 1836

Dear Jane

On the 20th of this month
thy Quarter was up and we have concluded to keep thee at home a while now,
but do not wish thee to forget what thee
has learned at School — I have heard thee
say a lesson every day since thee quit going
to School, and intend to continue doing so —
Thy brother Caleb goes to School to
Mary Hillman and her daughter Elizabeth
in Vine Street between 2d & 3d Street on the
North side — Thy sister Sarah I expect
will go to Haddonfield next week to stay
there awhile and go to School to your
Aunt Sarah who expects to teach a few
children this Summer — She has been very
much afflicted with lameness from a hurt
which she received from a fall about the
beginning of the year, and she has been
almost entirely confined to her room ever
since having been down stairs but once since —

There has been a War for some months past
in Florida between the Seminole Indians and
the Citizens of the United States, and it appears
probable there will be a war also with the
Creek Indians who inhabit a part of the States
of Georgia and Alabama, they having become
very troublesome of late and have committed
several murders and caused great terror &
distress among the white people who have
settled amongst them — It is a time of great
commotion in the Southern parts of the U S
and also on the Western part of Louisiana, as
there is a War raging at this time between
Mexico and one of her revolted provinces
called Texas which has set up for itself
and declared Independence — a great many
Citizens of the United States have gone to
help the Texians, and I am much afraid
this Country will be involved in War
with Mexico through their means —

Thy father J R Elfieth

Bill of Marketting bought in Callowhill
Street market. 8m 27th 1836 —

½ dozen Eggs @ 14cts 67
¼ peck Tomatoes 6c bunch of Beets 4 10
½ bushel round potatoes 31
3½ ℔ Sweet Potatoes 12½
½ peck String Beans 10
a pair of Chickens **50**
2 ℔ Butter @ 25cts 50
½ peck Apples 06
½ peck Peaches 20
a bunch of Smoked herrings 05
                                        ─────
                                        $2.01

Fruit generally this Summer is plenty and
cheap; but Watermelons are very Scarce
and dear — Plums, Peaches, Apples are
abundant and unusually sound and fair —
The Vegetable Market has been well Sup
plied — Tomatoes later this year than usual —
last week they were 12½cts a quarter of peck —
Some Jerseymen in our market between * John & 7th streets —

* Where 5m 2 1852 this place is now called Marshall street —

Within a short time so many elderly
persons have died that I think it worth
while to make a list of them, viz—

William Almy, Providence R.I. 2 m 5—1836 aged 75 Years
„ George Armroyd. Philadelphia 5 m 3 — „ —. 72
„ Barbara Boss „ 4 m 19 „ —. 75
„ William Cobbett — England 6 m 18—1835 „. 73
„ Cornplanter, the Indian Chief 2 m 7 1836 — „. 100
„ Joseph Cruikshank. Philadᵗ. 8 mo 9 — „ —. 89
„ Mary Clement (widow of Saml.) 2 m 27 „ —. 65
„ Sarah Champion — Haddonfield 5 m 16 — „ —. 74
D William Duane, Philadᵗ. — 11 m 24, 1835 „. 75
E Griffith Edwards, „ 3 m 5 1836 „. 82
F Walter Franklin, Lancaster 2 m 7 „ —. 62
„ Thomas Fassitt. Philadᵗ, 3 m 28 „. —. 59
„ Preston C Firth „ 10 m 4 1835 „. 65
„ William Folwell „ 11 m 3 — „ —. 76
G Frederick Gilbert „ 5 m 4 1836 „. 66
„ William Godwin — London 4 m 8 — „ —. 81
H Joseph Hatkinson — Philadᵗ 1 m 9 „ — 71
„ John Hunt — Darby 8 m 27 — „ — 83

Years

H Halliday Jackson Darby 2 m 9 1835 aged 63

I Thos. C James M.D. Philadr. 7 m 5 " — " 69

„ Joice Heth a black woman 2 m 19 – 1836 „ 162

K Jacob Knorr – Philadr. 11 m 25 – 1835 „ 76

„ Robert Kid – Burlington 8 m 17 – 1836 „ 73

L Joseph S Lewis – Philadr. 3 m 13 — „ — „ 57

„ Nathan Lippincott near Haddonfield 2 m 11 „ — „ 77

„ Edwd. Livingstone – N York 5 m 23 „ — „ 71

„ David Lapsley – Philadr. 8 m 18 „ — „ 92

M James Madison Virginia 6 m 28 — „ — „

„ Benjamin Masden Philadr. 4 m 6 „ — „ 65

„ John Moore M.D. „ — 5 m 22 „ — „ 58

„ Stephen Maxfield „ — 7 m 30 „ — „ 88

„ John Marshall, Chief Justice „ — 7 m 6 – 1835 „ —

O Sarah Osborne „ 4 m 9 — „ — „ 67

P Robert Poalk „ 4 m 4 1836 — „ 64

„ Hannah Pennell Darby 6 m 1 — „ — „ —

R William Rawle, Philadr. 4 m 12 — „ — „ 75

„ William Reed, West Chester 7 m 11 — „ — „ 55

„ Robert Ralston Philadr. 8 m 4 — „ — „ 74

S Abraham Sharples, Concord 9 m 21 – 1835 — „

„ Samuel J Smith, Burlington 10 m 14 — „ — „ 63

Thomas Shillitoe England 6 m 12 - 1836 aged 82

Wm. White, Bishop. Philad. 7 m 17 — " — " 88

Jacob Warren, Chairmaker " 8 m 7 — " — " 95

Robert Waln Philad. 1 m 24 — " — " 70

George Woolley — " — 2 m 5 — " — " 64

Peter Wiltberger — " — 5 m 18 - 1835 - " 73

Francis Wisely Concord 3 m 25 — " — " 82

John Wilson, M.D. Buckingham 10 m 15 — " — " 67

Mary Yarnall Philad. 2 m 27 - 1836 " 73

When I began this List I had no expectation it would be so long as it is. —

Moses Brown 9 m 6 . 1836 aged 98

Aaron Burr of New York 9 m 13 - " — " 81

Francis Boggs Philad. 9 m 17 — " — " 76

Thomas Shipley — " — 9 m 17 — " — " 48

Rachel Eastlack Newtown N J 8 m 25 " — " 52

Bohl Bohlen Philad. 10 m 10 — " — " 52

Conrad Keller — " 10 m 13 — " — " 84

John Mendenhall, Edgmonth 11 m 15 - " — " 88

[Tabitha Mendenhall " died 11 m 9 - 1845 aged 90]

Bill of Marketting bought 9 m 7 1836

1 pound Butter	.28½
1 pair Fowls	.62½
1 bushel Potatoes	.62½
½ peck Sweet potatoes	.12½
½ peck beans	.10
1 peck Apples	.12½
2 lb Smoked beef @ 12½ c	.25
Small Case 5 c pot herbs 1	06½
	$2.20

Ditto 9 m 24 th

1½ bushel Potatoes @ 62½ c	.94
1 lb Butter @ 37½ + 30	67½
1 quarter of Lamb	62½
1 peck Apples	16
½ peck Sweet potatoes	12½
½ peck beans	10
1 watermelon	10
Small Case	6
	$2.78½

Philadelphia 10 mo 27 a 1836
99

Dear Father

How is thee this Evening
I am much obliget to thee for that
borax that gave me this Evening it
has most made my mouth well
last night I made Caleb a baby
and I staid up till ten oclock
I dont know hardley what to say
I see that there is a letter for
mother; before this this is a very small
letter but I cant help it so farewell
for this time Thy Daughter
Jane Peirce Elyreth
Philad a 10 mo 29 th

Dear Mother

Aunt Mary Allen and
Cousin David came to see us on
the 27 t of this month, and we
were glad to see them.
Thy affectionate daughter
Sarah Elyreth &

121

100

Philad. 11 m 2. 1836

Dear Jane

I received thy short letter
this evening and was pleased with it —
After thee has been at School awhile with
thy Mother, I hope thee will write
better than thee now does —

Yesterday thy Aunt Elizabeth Elfrett
and Jacob Mull were here; they came
in a dearborn waggon and brought us
some apples out of my orchard at
Haddonfield — they are generally hard,
but very sound and look as if they
would keep well — Thee spent this
evening with me, and I helped thee
wind a skein of knitting cotton, and
thee sat by me knitting thy stocking
while I cut up some cabbages to pickle,
and held the light afterwards while
I salted them in the cellar —

This morning I bought 2 bushels of

122

mercer potatoes in Callowhill St. market
at 65 ct per bushel, and engaged the person
to bring 6 bushels more at the same price.
they are fine large potatoes — Saml. Archer
expects to leave here tomorrow for New
York with his wife and daughter to
take passage in a ship to Santa Cross
one of the West India Islands — I expect
they will get sail the next day, and
be absent about six months — They go
on account of his daughters health; she
has been very poorly several years with
Consumption, and they are in hopes she
will be benefitted by spending the
winter in a warmer climate — They
have no ice nor snow in the West Indies,
but the weather is warm there all
the year, and there are plenty of oranges
and pine apples there, and Cocoa nuts
also I believe — Farewell for to night
I remain thy affectionate father
Jacob R Elfreth —

Philad.ᵃ 11 m 3ᵈ. 1836

Dear little Sally

Thee has often walked in
Franklin Square and seen the grave yard
on the North side of the Square, with
a great many tomb stones, in it on
many of which there are inscriptions
and on some of them there are verses,
I remember seeing one which had on it,
"Sweet is the memory of the just,
"Twill flourish while they sleep in dust."
or something like that — Now I am going
to tell thee about this grave yard — It
has been in the possession of a Religious
Society of Germans for a great many years;
But William Penn when he laid out
the plan of Philadelphia, intended the
public Squares should be for the benefit
of the inhabitants of the city; and
when one of his sons gave this Society
the privilege of burying their dead in

this Square, he gave what did not belong to him — I suppose he thought it was a Lot of ground which would never be wanted for any thing else, as it was so far out of town, for at that time there were very few if any houses West of 4th Street —

When I was a boy there were not more than 10 or 12 houses in Wood Street, between 4th & 8th Streets, and what we now call Franklin Square was an open Lot except the burial ground, without any trees or handsome gravel walks in it — A few years ago the City Councils agreed to improve the Square, and they enclosed it with a wooden fence and planted trees in it and laid out the walks, and sowed it with grass seed, and as they did not like to have a grave yard in it, they tried to purchase of the German Society their supposed right to it, and I have been told they offered to

give them forty thousand dollars for it, but
the German Society wanted sixty thousand for
it, and as the City Councils were not willing
to give so much, the subject was taken to
Court, and after several years trial, it
has been decided that it belongs to the
City, and that the Society has no right to
it — Last year or the year before, the
City Councils began to enclose the Square
with a substantial iron palisade fence &
this fall they have completed it, having
removed the wooden fence on the North
side of the grave yard, and about three
weeks ago they took down the other fences
around it, so that the grave yard is
now open to any one who goes into the
Square — Some of the dead bodies have
been dug up, and removed by their
friends to another grave yard, and I
expect others will be; after which it
is probable the ground will be levelled

and laid out in walks and planted
with trees to correspond with the other
parts of the square — There is something
shocking in the idea of thus disturbing
the ashes of the dead, and if their
friends had refused to sell their supposed
right at any price I think it would
have been a very hard case to force it
from them and that it would have
been better to let them keep possession;
but as they were willing to sell provi-
-ded they got what they wanted for
it, this seems to alter the state of
the case, and I do not feel sorry
that what they were willing to sell
for money, they will now be deprived
of without any compensation whatever —

I have written thee a long letter
which, if thee should read it ten years
hence will be more interesting to thee
than it is now — Thy father Jacob R. E.

Philad^a 11 mo 4th

Dear Mother

How is thee to day
I believe thee is going to keep
school next weak – I have got
a sore hand which thee tied
up to day – Please to make us
some nice pumpkin pies –
I have read my hymn book
through – To be good is to be
happy – Joseph expects to go
to Mannington tomorrow –

Thy affectionate Son
Caleb P. Elfreth

Mother began to keep School on the
8th of the 11 month – The same
day George M Haverstick &
Sarah M. Whitall were
married at the North meeting.
John Mendenhall died 11 mo 15 1836 y^o 88

Philad. 11 mo 16th 1856.

Dear Jane

    This evening I heard of the death of Uncle John Mendenhall of Edgmont — He was an excellent, plain, honest man, "one of Natures noblemen." Such an one as the poet had in view when he wrote these lines,

"A wit's a feather, and a chief's a rod;
An honest man's the noblest work of God."

    Thee was at his house last summer on a visit, and I hope thee will long remember the last words he spoke to thee. "Be a good girl." I hope and believe he is now reaping the reward of a well spent life, and that he will enjoy a happy eternity, a never ending existence — He was born 6 mo 29th 1748, and was 88 years of age when he left this world for a better. —

    Thy affectionate father
        J R E —

Extract

The Rose and all its sweetness
Must wither and decay
But low my friend life's sweetness
May bear thy frame away
Though on thy Cheeks is blended
The Rose and Lily bloom
Death ere the day is ended
May bear thee to thy Tomb

Phila 12 mo 5th
1831

Dear Father
On the 15th of the 11 month
I went to George W Taylor
apprentice to the friend
to write envelops and
fold the Friend and
sell Books such as Bibles
and Testaments for 7/6 ts
I remain thy affectionate
son J R Elliott

Philadelphia 12 m 5 1836

Dear Father

Joseph has been writing thee
a letter. I it has been a long time since
I wrote to thee. How is thee thee is a cooking
some apples on the stove I dont now
hardley what to say cousin Rose, use
was at grand Fathers to supper and
Sarah and myself were there to tea
to Joseph my cousin Jesse went to the museum
to naght after supper I believe I must
leave off for this time so farewell Thy affectionate
Daughter   Jane P Elyth

Dear Jane   Philad. 12 m 8 1836

I received thy letter and read
it with pleasure, as I always love to see
my children improving themselves in
letter writing which is a pretty and a
useful part of education — Last sixth
day evening the 2d of this month Mary

Cowgill died suddenly at the house
of her nephew Charles West in Arch street.
She had just returned from the Western
Country where she had been on a visit
to her friends — She was found dead on
the floor having fallen backwards, and
it is probable she died immediately —

 This evening I heard of the death
of our worthy friend Othniel Alsop — he
died this afternoon — It is but a few
days since we both heard him preaching
at our Meeting in New Street, where
we have often seen and heard him —
I believe he was a good and a useful
man, and I hope we shall profit by
the good advice he often gave us — He
was an Englishman by birth but came
to this Country when he was a young
man, with his brother John Alsop —

 He was a Merchant at one time,
but of late years he has been a

Manufacturer of Vinegar, and had a
Counting house in Vine Street between Crown
and 5th Street adjoining his vinegar yards,
which extended from Vine to Wood Street
nearly opposite to where thee was born—

Yesterday afternoon I walked up
to Haddonfield to see my Sister Sarah
who is still confined to the house with
the hurt she received by a fall in
the 1st Month of this year— I left her
more poorly this morning than I found
her; She had a turn of her old Complaint last night, the disease of the
heart, to which she has long been
subject— I returned by the Stage
to day in Company with our friend
Elizabeth Edwards who came to pay a
visit in Philad. and I hope she
will come to see us before she returns—
There was a good deal of ice in the river—
Thy affectionate father J R Elfreth

112 Philadelphia 12 m 30 c 1836

Dear Father

How is thee this
evening? I thought I would write thee
a letter this evening. thee bought
Mother some oysters cooked some
of them and left the others
for another time and thee gave
Sally and Caleb and Maysely some
of them raw, and they were frozen,
and we were much obliged to thee
for thee is very kind I know
for thee gives us a good many things
we dont deserve more than the
little beggars, and the poor folks
such as Susen Brown who came
here to day, and she said that
she had not a stick of wood to
her name nor stove to put fire
in, and she said she did not
want to beg. and I hope we

we will not forget the poor.
we are all well but Caleb. and
he had. the sore throat. and
Mother was not well. and I
have had the head ache. I beleive
I have said enough at present
so farewell — Thy Daughter
Jane P Everett 1836,

Dear Mother. This is the first day
of the week & the first day of the
month & the first day of the year
& I think we all ought to be better
and Love & Praise him who made
us & be thankful to him for All
the good things he gives us & I tho't
like to be a great deal better than
I am. I would be very much
obliged to the for some nutlongs
but I remain thy son
1 mo 1830 J Everett

A Prayer

"Thou friend of my childhood
 And guide of my youth:
Thou Father of mercy,
 And fountain of Truth!
Protect and direct me
 Wherever I stray,
And bless little Caleb
 Each hour of the day.
When up in the morning
 I rise from my bed.
Oh! let thy kind angels
 Be plac'd o'er my head. —
And when at my tasks
 My School, or my play;
Still bless little Caleb
 Each hour in the day. —
When night spreads its shades
 O'er the waves of the deep.
And Caleb is sunk
 In the stillness of sleep,

O still let thy poor child
  Be dear in thy sight,
And bless little Caleb
  Each hour in the night."

Philadᵃ 1 mo 6 1857

Dear Children

There was a dreadful
Shipwreck near New York last third
day Morning — The Brig Mexican 70 days
from Liverpool went on Shore, and out
of 116 persons on board only 8 were Saved —
The others all perished; many of them
it is supposed had frozen to death &
the others were drowned — It is said
the Brig arrived in sight of land on
first day evening and made signals for
a pilot and also signals of distress, being
short of provisions, but no one came to their
assistance until they struck the beach & then
only one boat load was taken off —

137

116

Philad. 1 mo 17 1837.

This day we had the company of our much esteemed friend Stephen Grellet at the North Meeting — In his communication he repeated many passages from Scripture, among others the following from the 51 Chapter of Isaiah "Hearken to me ye that follow after right=eousness, ye that seek the Lord: look unto the rock whence ye are hewn, and to the hole of the pit whence ye are digged. —

Hearken unto me, ye that know righteous=ness, the people in whose heart is my law; fear ye not the reproach of men, neither be ye afraid of their revilings. For the Moth shall eat them up like a garment, and the worm shall eat them like wool" — In the Preparative meeting the case of George Dilks' application for reception into membership was acted upon, and directed to be taken to the Monthly meeting — Edward Randolph & Jeremiah Willets visited him from the Prep. meeting —

Philad.ᵃ Nov 29th 1837

Dear Children

On the evening of the 25th inst.
we had an opportunity of seeing a most
splendid exhibition of the Aurora Borealis —
It began between 6 & 7 o'clock and continued
until 10 — The Northern part of the heavens
extending to the East and West seemed to
be covered with a coat of living fire,
while beautiful streaks of pale light
shot up from the horizon to the zenith
and even farther South, meeting in a
common centre near the Pleiades and
curling round in a beautiful manner —
The prevailing colour was red of various
hues, scarlet, pink & cherry, and the
forms and shapes were constantly changing —
The larger stars and the beautiful planets
Jupiter and Mars were visible through this
fiery cloud and the moon after it rose,
but they all appeared of a deep red colour —
You all had the privilege of seeing

this magnificent Spectacle except James and
his youngest Sister who were in bed — I wish
you to talk about it and remember it,
for it is not probable you will ever see
the like again — The Delaware has
been frozen over several weeks, and people
Cross it with horses and Sleighs, and Some
haul wood from Jersey to Philadelphia
on the ice — This is a wonderful bridge
and made in a wonderful manner —
If Cold acted upon water as it does
upon almost all other bodies, by dim-
inishing their bulk and increasing their
weight, ice as it became formed would
Sink to the bottom of the river, and so
in time the whole body of water
would become solid, which would destroy
the fish and all other animated beings
which inhabit it; but that Divine Being
who cares for the meanest of his creatures
has ordered it otherwise, and by a

wonderful provision has made water to increase in bulk after it is cooled to a certain extent, by which means the ice being lighter than the liquid water, floats upon its surface, and the fish swim about as usual though nearer to the bottom of the rivers than before.— The Aurora Borealis is supposed to be produced by electricity, which being formed near the north pole that is constantly covered with ice, and of course prevents it from being conducted into the earth; it shoots upwards in those beautiful streams of light and plays about, until as it bends over the earth where the cold is not so great it gradually mixes with the surrounding air and disappears.—

Last evening I took Jane to hear a lecture on anatomy by Dr. Pancoast.— The subject of his lecture was digestion which was very interesting to a large audience.—

Your affectionate father

Jacob R Elfreth

141

120

Philad.ª 1m 30 - 1837

Dear Joseph

I was pleased to find last
sixth day evening, thee had become so
expert in folding Newspapers — Thee folded
seven quires of the "Friend" in 35 minutes,
each paper being folded over four times —
when exerting thyself to the utmost, thee
folded 8 papers in a minute at one
time, and several times thee folded
7 in a minute — I wish thee to not
be satisfied with this, but try to do
thy work in the least possible time;
for as thee only has a certain quantity
to do, thee will then have more leisure
for improving in thy learning — But above
all things my son remember "The fear
of the Lord is the beginning of Wisdom,
and to depart from evil is understanding"
Be dutiful and obedient to all that are
placed over thee, and subdue thy temper —
                    Thy father J R E

Dear Jane,   Philad.ᵃ 2 mo 6ᵗʰ 1837

Within the last fortnight I have
taken them twice to hear lectures on Anatomy
by Doctor Pancoast at the Friends Reading
Rooms Corner of Greenleaf or Appletree alley
and 4ᵗʰ Street — He told us the heat of
the Stomach was about 100° — The time
employed in digestion is about four hours
and a half — The entrails leading from the
Stomach is 40 feet in length, and the surface
of it would be sufficient to cover a large
table, or the human body all over —
The weight of blood in a grown person
is supposed to be about 35 pounds ; the
motion of the heart drives it through the
arteries to all parts of the body, and
it is returned again to the heart by
the veins ; a quantity of blood equal to
the whole amount or 35 pounds is passed
through the heart every three minutes —
Water taken into the Stomach remains there
only about 20 minutes before it is taken up

by the absorbents and enters into the blood,
so that it is not necessary to drink a great
deal of water to assist digestion — He might
have told us if he had thought proper, that
the water which we drink is mixed with
the blood before it passes from the body
in the form of perspiration, urine &, for
such is the fact —

On the first of this month I paid $12 =
for a barrel of wheat flour —

By a statement in the "Globe" it appears
the Florida War has cost the United
States about five millions of dollars —
If one half of that sum had been
expended towards the improvement of
the poor Indians how much more good
might have been done — but "the wages
of sin are death", and "the way of the
transgressor is hard" — human policy often
costs more than it is worth and sometimes
it is defeated after all its endeavours —

At our Quarterly Meeting to day which
was held in the East end of Arch street
Meeting house, It was Concluded to hold
the next meeting in the 5th month in the
West End of the house — The Men & women
are to meet there together, and after holding
a Meeting for worship, the Women are to withdraw
into the East room and hold their meeting
there; I suppose the Men would have had
gallantry enough to go there themselves if
it was not that the Women have no means
of going out of doors to get into their meeting
room — The river delaware is still
frozen over and wood is drawn across
it on sleds, but in consequence of the
Mildness of the weather it is thought to
be unsafe as the ice must have been
considerably weakened during the last few
days — We heard of the arrival to day
at New York. of the ship Covington & that
some goods on board for Richard Oakford —
Thy affection to father — J R Elbkth

124

Philad. 2 m 21 1837

Dear James

I have just returned from
Monthly Meeting held in Key's alley —
George Dilks was received a member
this day — We were informed the
Lot of Ground belonging to Friends
bounded by Arch & Filbert Streets and
by Schuylkill 4th & 5th Streets has been
sold for $72,000 — A Lot at the corner
of 6th & Noble Street has been purchased
for $28,500. Whereon there is to be
erected a new Meeting house for the
accomodation of Friends of Northern
District Monthly meeting — The
Committee appointed to make Collections
reported that they had attended to it
& paid into the hands of the Treasurer
including his subscription $1368 25/100 —
Shew this letter to thy mother —

Thy affe father J R E

146

"Give to him that asketh thee; and from
him that would borrow of thee, turn
not thou away. Matt V. 42

———

Oh stay not thy hand when the winter winds rude,
  Blow cold through the dwelling of want & despair
To ask if misfortune has come to the good,
  Or if folly has wrought the wreck that is there.
When the heart-stricken wanderer asks thee for bread,
  In suffering he bows to necessity's laws;
When the wife moans in sickness — the children unfed —
  The cup must be bitter — oh ask not the cause.
When the Saviour of men raised his finger to heal
  Did he ask if the sufferer was Gentile or Jew?
When thousands were fed, was the bountiful meal
  To be given alone to the faithful and true? —
Then scan not too closely the frailties of those
  Whose bosoms may bleed in the cold winter's day
But give to the friendless who tells thee his woes,
  And from him that would borrow, oh turn not away.
                        O. C. H.

———

From the Philadᵃ Gazette 2 nov. 1836 —

Character of Christ.

Behold where in a mortal form,
　Appears each grace divine:
The virtues, all in Jesus met,
　With mildest radiance shine.
The noblest love of human kind
　Inspir'd his holy breast;
In deeds of mercy, words of peace,
　His kindness was exprest.
To spread the rays of heavenly light,
　To give the mourner joy,
To preach glad tidings to the poor,
　Was his divine employ.
Lowly in heart, by all his friends,
　A friend and servant found;
He wash'd their feet, he wip'd their tears,
　And heal'd each bleeding wound.
Midst keen reproach, and cruel scorn,
　Patient and meek he stood:
His foes, ungrateful, sought his life;
　He labour'd for their good.

In the last hour of deep distress,
   Before his Father's throne,
With soul resign'd, he bow'd and said,
   "Thy will, not mine, be done!"
Be Christ my pattern and my guide!
   His image may I bear!
O may I tread his sacred steps:
   And his bright glories share.

                              Enfield

———

Should my Children read this after
my head is laid in the silent grave,
let them remember that it was their
father's most anxious desire for them that
they might look to Christ for their
pattern and their guide, and endeavour
to tread in his sacred steps; obey his
precepts and commandments, and in
all their actions do that which they
think will be pleasing in his sight —
Then, after they leave this world they
will live with him forever —
   Philad. Dec 27. 1837 —   JRE

Some Memorandums — Martin Van Buren the President of the United States went into office 3m 4 1837 — He was elected by the People, or in other words a majority of the Electors chosen by the People of the several States voted for him — There were several other Candidates, viz Daniel Webster of Massachusetts, William Harrison of Ohio, and Judge White of Florida or some of the Southern States I believe — None of the Candidates of the Office of Vice President had a majority of the Electors so it went to the Senate, which elected Richard M Johnson — The House of Representatives ended their Session on the morning of 3m 4th after passing very few Bills of importance —
The new Senate had a short Session on and after the 4th of 3m month and approved the nomination of George M Dallas of this City as Minister to Russia, and Polwhattan Ellis as Minister to Mexico — 3m 13 1837 —

The effects of over trading and excessive
Speculation appears to be in a train of
disclosing itself in such a way, that the
monetary institutions of this Country will
be shaken from Maine to Georgia and from
the Atlantic to the Pacific — A few days
since we heard of the failure of 3 houses in
New Orleans whose responsibilities amounted
to 6 or 7 millions of dollars (Herman &c)
and a day or two after the house of Joseph
& brother in New York for about $5,000,000 and
Yesterday that of Philips for several millions
more — These are all Jews I believe, but
the credit of some of our other merchants
and great land Speculators is Shaken, and
we may expect to hear in a day or two
of their giving way — Fryer & Anderson who
stopped payment on the 18th of this month
their debts are said to amount to $600,000.
I hope and believe the Country at large will
be benefitted in the end — 3 mo 21 — 1837 —

The way to be happy

A hermit there was,
  And he liv'd in a grot,
And the way to be happy,
  They said he had got.
As I wanted to learn it,
  I went to his cell
And when I came there,
  The old hermit said "Well,
Young man, by your looks,
  You want something I see,
Now tell me the business
  That brings you to me.
The way to be happy
  They say you have got
And as I want to learn it
  I've come to your grot.
Now I beg and entreat
  If you have such a plan
That you'll write it me down
  As plain as you can."

Upon which the old hermit
 Went to his pen,
And brought me this note
 When he came back again.
"Tis Being, and Doing
 And Having, that make
All the pleasures and pains
 Of which we partake.
To Be what God pleases —
 To Do a man's best,
And to Have a good heart —
 Is the way to be blest." —

———

4 Mo — 15 — 1837 This afternoon, Caleb and
Sarah and James went to Haddenfield
to stay during the week of the Yearly
Meeting — I took them over the river
and saw them safely in the Stage —
I expect they will spend a very
pleasant week if the weather should
be pleasant and they keep well —

132   John Peirson _ died at
Leamington, Warwickshire England on
the 18th of 1st month 1837 in the 46th year
of his age. _ His complaint was Con=
=sumption of the lungs, which had been
gradually gaining ground for the last
eighteen months. He was enabled
through the mercy of Him who died
for us, to bear his sufferings with great
patience often appearing very desirous
that his will might be brought into
entire subjection to the will of his
dear Redeemer. Not long before
the final close, reviving a little from
an alarming difficulty of respiration,
it was observed to him that he seemed
better; "Yes," he replied, "but I thought
I saw the face of Jesus, and it was so
pleasant I did not want to come back
again". _ again _ "I have nothing to trust but
the mercies of my dear Saviour" _

the "Friend" 4 mo 15 _ 1837 _

Philadelphia Yearly Meeting of Friends
began 4m 17-1837- The Representatives from
the different Quarterly Meetings were called
over - There are ten Quarterly Meetings viz.
Philadelphia, Abington, Bucks, Concord,
Caln, Western, Burlington, Haddonfield
Salem, Shrewsbury & Rahway -- The
Epistles from other yearly Meetings were read
and a Committee appointed to answer them -

In the Afternoon, the Minutes of the
Meeting for Sufferings were read & a very
interesting Address to the People of the
United States on the Subject of the
descendents of Africa & the Aborigines
or Indians of this Country -

3d day 4m 18th. The Queries were read
& Answers from the different Meetings
which occupied the 1st sitting & part of
the afternoon - It was concluded to
discontinue the Meeting at Charleston S.C.
where there is but 1. Member & only 2

134

others who have been in the practice of attend
ing that meeting for a considerable time past —
Our venerable friend John Cox attended
both sittings this day & was very lively
in speaking to business this morning — He is
one of the excellent of the earth ——
He made some observations upon the pernicious
effects of reading works of the imagination
with which the press of the County may
be said to be groaning under at this time
I hope his remarks will be beneficial to
myself and to many others ——
4th day 4 Mo 19th I was not at the morning
sitting to day, but was told the Report
of the Boarding School at West Town was
read, by which it appears the income
fell short of the expenses the last year
by upwards of $12.00 to each Scholar —
In the afternoon sitting it was proposed
that the actual expenses of those children
who are paid for out of the fund for

Schooling poor Friends children, should be charged to this fund, and as there are now about 30 of that class in the School, it will amount to more than $360 — besides the regular charge of 68 dollars for annum for each.

It was also proposed to have a Summer and Winter Session so that the Schollars may be entered at the commencement of each Session in order to their better classification, and that there should be a recess between the Sessions, of 3 weeks in the Spring and 2 weeks in the Autumn in order that the Teachers might have an opportunity to recruit their health & strength — Both of these Propositions were adopted by the Meeting, the latter of which is to be carried into effect next fall or in the 10th month —

On the subject of the first Proposition a few friends were opposed to it, and their sentiments on that subject were like my own —

5th day 4 Mo 20th This Morning, Meetings for worship were held at the different Meeting house but I did not get to attend one, as my employer was engaged at Court on a Jury — neither did I go to the afternoon setting as I could not leave my business until it was past the hour the meeting adjourned to — I believe the Report of the Committee on the Indians was read this afternoon —

6th day 4 Mo 21 — I was not at the setting this morning and do not know what was done, but I attended the last setting which was held this afternoon — The Essays of the Epistles to the different Yearly Meetings were read viz to Rhode Island, New York, Baltimore, Virginia, North Carolina, Ohio, Indiana, Dublin, and London — After which the Minutes were read, a very solemn pause ensued and the Yearly Meeting Concluded, to meet at the usual time next year if the Lord permit —

In one of the sittings of the Yearly meeting
a young Man from Virginia addressed the meeting
at considerable length upon the subject of the
degraded situation of the free people of
Colour in this City, and recommending that
Means should be taken to elevate them in
the estimation of Society and to remove the
great weight of prejudice that exists towards
them at present — I have since been told
his name is Henry Granger, he was a
considerable Slave holder before he became
a Member of our Society, and liberated
Slaves to the value of $40,000 — It seems
his mind was directed to the iniquity of
Slavery by the example of a public Friend
who put up at his house some years ago
and felt scrupulous about partaking of
the food on his table because it was the
produce of Slave labour — I believe this
friends name was Margaret Allinson —

138

Phila – 5 mo 11th 1837

Dear Mother

The Banks in this city
suspended specie payments to day
and those of New York stopped
payment yesterday – I dont know
what we are to do for silver
money to go to market with,
but Father thinks there will
be some way provided, so that
we shall have food and
raiment —

D S. 0022   Philad 5th mo 23 1842

Dear father how does thee
do James was sick the
day he went in the country,
And puked a good eal he was
Better the next day And plaid
a good eal

So fair well thy affectionate R P Elfreth

Philadᵃ 7mo 24ᵗʰ 1837

Dear Caleb,

On the 18 of this month. the
Ship Washington arrived from
Calcutta. having on board a
8 Chimpanzees. Ourang Outang.
& severall Boa Constrictors.
On the Same day. the Ship of the
Line Pennsylvania. was launched.
this is Supposed to be one of the
largest Ships in the World.
And it has been 15 Years since
the Keel was Laid. Aunt Mary
Allen paid us a visit last Week.
and Went out to West Town to
see her daughter Hannah she
went home last seventh day.
and thee Went with her. And
I expect thee is enjoying thyself
finely. I my affectionate

Brother Jos. H. E. Speed

161

Philada 10mo 14 1837

Dear Father

The Franklin Square has been much Improved this year. The Grave yard on the north side has been levelled, and laid out in gravel walks. Some of the dead bodies were dug up and removed by their friends. most of the tomb stones are burried under the gravel walks. The square has been lighted with gas, And they are now engaged in constructing a Fountain in the centre of the square with a large and costly marble basin which when finished I expect will be very ornamental. ——

Last evening there was a total eclipse of the moon the sky was clear and we had a fine veiw of it. Caleb is marking a mock orange for a globe. Mother and Joseph have been to grand Fathers this evening and have just returned. there was ice this morning.

Thy affectionate Daughter
Jane P. Elfreth

Philadᵃ 10 mo 20ᵗʰ 1837

My dear Mother

How is thee this evening?
I am going to write thee a letter —
On the 7ᵗʰ 8ᵗʰ & 9ᵗʰ of this month
there was a tremendous N E Storm
off the Coast of North Carolina —
The Steam boat Home was run
ashore near Cape Hateras, went to
pieces and 95 persons perished —
Uncle Samuel Allen came here
this evening and brought us some
hops and a cheese, and Aunt
Mary sent mother some yarn
to make us stockings — I think
they are very kind and we
are obliged to them
I remain
thy little
daughter
Sarah Elfreth

142

Philad.. 11 mo 17th 1837

Andrew Jackson Harvey
        Dear Friend
                How is thee?
Please send me my Squirter –
I dont know what to tell thee
hardly – We have had a Snow
Storm last 3rd. day and there is
snow on the houses stile –
    Since I was at Mannington
we have got another little
brother his name is Jacob
and he was born 10 mo 22d. –
    The nurse who gave him to
Mother said she got him in
Jersey where they are as
thick as blackberries – .
    Please to give my love to
Uncle and Aunt & Cousins –
        Thy little friend
    Caleb Greth 11 m 19 o 10 37

Public Ministry of Friends

"We do not hesitate to admit, not only that the services of rightly appointed and qualified Ministers may receive a particular character from their several habits of thought & expression, but also that they may be found at times more or less marked by their peculiar infirmities, and attended by other indications of human frailty and imperfection.

Such things may well humble us, and teach us not to overrate the spiritual gifts and attainments of our fellow-men; but they afford no ground whatever for calling in question the reality of an immediate spiritual guidance and qualification for the work of the ministry. —

If our own spirits are rightly exercised in regard to that which may be offered by our brethren or sisters, I believe we shall sometimes be made sensible, to our instruction and edification that the service

service in which they have been engaged
has not been performed in their own will,
but at the bidding of their divine Master,
even though they may have used some
expressions of which we do not approve. —
But if, instead of such an exercise as this,
we give way to a critical and captious
spirit, our intellectual faculties may
indeed be sharpened, but our spiritual
perception will be in danger of becoming
dim, and our strength, far from receiving
increase, will be likely to decay". —

Extracts from the "Friends" Vol 11ᵗʰ page 46 —

Philad⁴ 12 mo 14 1835

Dear Father
              Thee has been out
to see about Joseph Scooling I beleive
I thought I would write to thee this evening
as it has been a long time since I have wrote
to thee. Sis Sarah and me have been talking
about cristmas things or toys I should say
and I will put down a list of the things
we want thee to buy us If thee please this
is it   list of cristmas things
    Rebecca a little table 6 cts chest 3 cts
    James a little coffepot and kettle
  Sarah a little table & looking glass
Jane a little Stand 12 cts please get us a
6 cts worth of little leaden chairs which are
a cent a peice. please excuse bad
writing as pens were not good. Joseph has
been to haddonfield and has come
back again. farewell for this
time thy affectionate Daughter Jane Earl

146

Philad^a 12 mo 4 1837

Dear Mother

I thought I would
write to thee — Joseph began to day
to go to school to John H. Millite
in Zane street above 7th street.

I quit going to school last 7th
day, Mother thinks it will be
two cold for me to go this winter
Jane and Caleb continue going
to school to Lydia T. Reeve in
4th street above Callowhile street.

We talked about James going
to school, but I believe he is
not going until Spring —

Farewell for to night
Thy little daughter
Sarah Elfreth

Latin Numbers for Jane P Elfreth

Unus — 1.	Primus — 1st first	
Duo — 2.	Secundus 2nd	
Tres — 3.	Tertius — 3d	
Quatuor 4.	Quartus — 4th	
Quinque 5.	Quintus — 5th	
Sex — 6.	Sextus — 6th	
Septem 7.	Septimus 7th	
Octo — 8.	Octavus — 8th	
Novem 9.	Nonus — 9th	
Decem — 10.	Decimus — 10th	
Undecim 11.	Undecimus 11th	
Duodecim 12.	Duodecimus 12th	
Tredecim 13.	Decimus tertius 13th	
Quatuordecim 14.	Decimus quartus 14th	
Quindecim 15.	Decimus quintus 15th	
Sexdecim 16.	Decimus sextus — 16th	
Septendecim 17.	Decimus septimus 17th	
Octodecim — 18.	Decimus octavus 18th	
Novendecim 19.	Decimus nonus — 19th	
Viginti — 20	Vicesimus } — 20th	
	or Vigesimus }	over

169

Semel	—	once	Singuli —	one by one
Bis,	—	twice	Bini —	2 by 2
Ter,	—	thrice or 3 times	Terni —	3 by 3
Quater	—	4 times	Quaterni —	4 by 4
Quinquies	—	5 times	Quini —	5 by 5
Sexies	—	6 times		
Septies	—	7 times		
Octies	—	8 times		
Novies	—	9 times		
Decies	—	10 times		
Undecies	—	11 times		
Duodecies		12 times		
Tredecies	—	13° times		
Quatuordecies.		14 times		
Quindecies	—	15 times		
Sexdecies	—	16 times		
Decies ac Septies		17 times		
Decies ac Octies		18 times		
Decies ac novies	—	19 times		
Vicies	—	20 times		
Vicies ac Semel		21 times		

Philad.ᵃ 12 mo 25ᵗʰ 1837

My dear Mother

This day is called Christmas: it is celebrated by a great many pious people as the day of the nativity of our blessed Saviour Jesus Christ who left the bosom of his Father and came into the world to save sinners. "For God so loved the world that he gave his only begotten Son that whosoever believeth in him should not perish but have everlasting life".—

We ought to love this dear Saviour and try to please him and then we shall love one another and be kind, and try to please one another.—

Farewell for to night

Thy affectionate daughter

Sarah Elfreth Jun.

Philad^a 12 mo 31 1837

Dear Father
and Mother,

How are you?
This is the last day of 1837
and our letter book is nearly
filled. I thought I would
write to you this evening, it
has been a long time since I
received a letter from either of
you — James has gone to bed
and Jane has gone to Grandfathers
and Joseph to meeting —

Farewell for to night your

birth daughter

Sarah Elfreth

Jesus sought me when a stranger
Wandering from the fold of God
He to rescue me from danger
Interposed his precious blood

Jane P Elfreth

172

Philad.ᵃ 12 m. 31. 1857

My dear Children

The year is fast drawing to its
close, and another day will be the beginning
of another year — How have you spent your
time during the last twelve months? are
you wiser than you were twelve months ago
If you are, then you must be better; for
"the fear of the Lord is the beginning of
Wisdom". — You all know more than you did
a year ago, but knowledge is not wisdom.
The poet of the New Testament as Cowper
has been called, says.
"Knowledge and Wisdom far from being one,
Have ofttimes no Connexion, —
Knowledge is proud that he has learned so much —
Wisdom is humble that she knows no more."
It is a common thing at this season of the year
to express good wishes, and to make acceptable
presents to the young persons in particular — You
have had your presents, and now I am going

express my wishes for you, in which I doubt not
your dear Mother will join with me —

for Joseph I wish he may become more patient
of things which cross his own will, more careful
in his personal appearance, more diligent in
his studies. — for Jane I wish she may
become more patient in her disposition, more
affectionate to her brothers and sisters, and more
helpful to her Mother. — for Caleb I wish
he may become more patient of contradiction,
retain his love of reading, and by cultivating
brotherly love get rid of selfishness —.
for Sarah, I wish she may become faster
in her movements, fonder of her books, and
continue her disposition to be kind to her
brothers and sisters and domestic in her habits. —
for James, I wish he may learn to speak
plainer, and always be careful to speak
the truth — for Rebecca I wish she may get
well of the tetter, and always be as careful
to keep things in their right places as she is

now — for my little namesake, I wish he
may always sleep as well at night as he
does now, and that his Mother & himself
may be spared the pain and trouble which
attends a child afflicted with the latter —

For all of you my dear Children, I wish
you may grow in grace as you grow in years,
that you may be dutiful to your parents, kind
to each other affectionate to your relatives and
friends, and benevolent in your dispositions, and
beneficent according to your means towards the
whole human family — That you may not
give way to anger, but always endeavour
when you are wronged to overcome evil with
good — That as you grow older you may also
become more dilligent in all that is good. &
Finally that when we are done with the things of
this world we may all meet together a happy
family in the world which is to come —

    Your affectionate father
        Jacob R Elfreth

Afterword

Although the *Book of Letters* concludes in the year 1837, all of the Elfreth children outlived their parents and spent their adulthoods in the Philadelphia area.

Despite Jacob's objections, Abigail Elfreth and her father negotiated an apprenticeship for Joseph with linen merchants Randolph and Richardson in 1840. He did not remain in their employ for long, however, and moved to Haddonfield, New Jersey, in 1852. Shortly after his arrival, he married Hannah Hill and the couple had three children. Joseph is listed as a salesman in Camden directories; he died in the fall of 1898, at the age of seventy-four.

Jane married Dr. James Morris Corse in the Sixth Street Meeting House in 1858 and had two children. The Corses lived in what is now known as the University City area for many years; after the death of her husband in 1885 until her own death in 1912, Jane lived with her son, James Corse, on North 39th Street.

Caleb begame a druggist and speculated in city real estate. He and Anna M. Shepherd married in 1855 and had seven children. Of all the diarists, Caleb seems to have met with the most financial success during his lifetime, for he owned six houses in Philadelphia when he died in February 1909.

Sarah Elfreth never married and lived with her mother after Jacob's death in 1870. She was particularly close to her sister Mary throughout her life, and left all her "table linens and bed quilts" to her sister when she died in Delaware County in April 1885, at the age of fifty-five.

All of the diarists were buried in area Quaker graveyards.

THE ELFRETH BOOK OF LETTERS

Edited, with an Introduction, by SUSAN WINSLOW HODGE

Foreword by Anthony N. B. Garvan

In 1835 Jacob R. Elfreth purchased a small blank book for his four children to write in frequently. This facsimile edition of their letters will charm and delight everyone with its intimacy. ¶ One can see Jane sitting next to her mother, mending in the evening by lamp and fire, as she writes about her day. The day young Joseph describes with his mother in bed after childbirth and the kitchen chimney on fire resembles days in all of our lives. ¶ The children's view of early American life illuminates the daily rigors, but the overall impression one takes from the book is the love within the family and the steadfast Quaker belief in learning. ¶ Joseph, Caleb, Jacob, and Jane were to write often of events from cousins for dinner to an assassination attempt on President Andrew Jackson. And, as their writing became more polished, their penmanship much improved, and they learned to write by quill without smearing the ink, we see them grow up. Their father also wrote in the book of trips they took and events of the day. ¶ The Elfreth family was prominent in Philadelphia; indeed the name of their predecessor graces Elfreth's Alley, a carefully preserved and nurtured row of houses four blocks from Independence Hall, the oldest residential area occupied without interruption in America. Students of early American and social history will find the book as enlightening as it is delightful. ¶ This book was funded by the Elfreth's Alley Association, Inc., and the Quaker Chemical Foundation as part of the Association's fiftieth anniversary celebration. ¶ SUSAN WINSLOW HODGE is Curator of the Elfreth's Alley Museum.

Cover Design: Adrianne Onderdonk Dudden

Cover: "Winter Scene on the Delaware," by P. S. Duval.
Reproduced with permission of The Historical Society of Pennsylvania.

UNIVERSITY OF PENNSYLVANIA PRESS

Blockley Hall, 418 Service Drive upp *Philadelphia, Pennsylvania 19104*

ISBN 0-8122-1208-8